TANDEN REVOLUTION

TANDEN REVOLUTION

SCOTT MEREDITH

See Otter Books

Published by See Otter Books

ISBN 978-1-9840-1371-2

Typesetting services by BOOKOW.COM

To the memory of the master Tai Chi 'jeweler',
WANG ZONGYUE
王宗岳
who first cut, polished, and set Tai Chi —
the mysteriously radiant gem.

~ ~ ~

To the greatest Tai Chi master
of his generation,
BENJAMIN PANG JENG LO
羅邦楨
who is in no way responsible
for any part of this wild book.

ACKNOWLEDGMENTS

The author is grateful for the invaluable assistance of Thomas Campbell and Sean Compton in the preparation of this book.

CONTENTS

Chapter 1

INTRODUCTION

"*All Scott's books are a bit repetitive.*"
  - Amazon.co.uk customer review

"*If one child gives the effect another turn of the screw, what do you say to two children?*"
"*We say, of course,*" somebody exclaimed, "*that they give two turns! Also that we want to hear about them.*"
  - Henry James, 'The Turn of the Screw'

"*Through repetition the wise man is sure to attain mastery of the mantra.*"
  - Shivasamhita

Repetitive? *Hell yes.* That's the nature of the art. In this book I'm not just going to *repeat* the fundamentals – I'm going to *rub your nose in them.* Our monkey minds always want something newer, better, a gleamier bauble dangled in our face. Forget that. The classical internal model doesn't work that way. It's repetition all the way down. It's lifelong, consistent grinding on the basics. You should be *thanking* me for telling you openly and honestly that you don't need yet another 100-move form or a secret internal *neidan* meditation (with a chart of VLSI circuit diagram complexity). Repetition that looks simple on the surface masks incredible profundity in the depths. But you have to base your work correctly.

There's always room for refinement That's not adding novelty in our gross physical moves, but upping our *understanding*, and pointing out new vistas in the *experience* that results from all the repetition. I have plenty more twists and insights to offer in that mode, and that's what this book is about.

This book is based on the ARC model of human internal energy. ARC stands for:

1. *Accumulate* (or *Activate*) energy - in abdomen
2. *Rebound* energy - from feet
3. *Catch* energy - with hands

I've gone over lots of details and drills on this in other books, but I'm not setting those books as prerequisite for this one. The ARC idea is straightforward and simple enough to pick up as you go. The energy is an accessible, tangible thing that you can learn to work with as directly as dribbling a basketball. It just takes practice. I'll be talking about the ARC throughout this book. Even if you aren't familiar with it from my past works, just ride with the flow. You'll be able to follow the practices perfectly well. Once you start to feel it for yourself, you won't need a weatherman to tell you how the wind blows.

In the previous books, I've tried to simplify the internal training process. I want to scale it back to the bare bones basics. From hundreds of feedback reports received, I'd say that's worked out pretty well. However, some of the questions I get are leading me to think maybe I've assumed too much. Maybe I skimmed too lightly over some essential fundamentals. I tend to think certain things are easier to grok than my readers have found them to be. Effects that came to me early on, from personal instruction under my teachers, seem to be more difficult to access remotely through my books.

In this book, I want to go over the foundational stuff with a fine tooth comb. It will seem repetitive because it deals with exactly the same concepts and energy models I've presented all along. I'm using much the same terminology and I've even reproduced some graphics that have previously appeared. But for those who've tried to work seriously with the existing material, this book should be a gold mine and a godsend because I'm going way deeper down the operational rabbit hole this time around. The key thing is to feel it, work it, and own it for yourself. Anyone who's used these methods to experience the internal energy knows – *it rocks so hard!* Once you've really felt it, you wouldn't grudge me the price of one, two, a dozen, or a hundred books putting it out there.

What would be something *new*? Look at the chart showing just one of *seven* beginner-level Seven-Star Praying Mantis forms, all of which I learned and practiced intensively in my teens. All seven of these are nearly 100 moves each. Would that qualify as *something new*? Is that what you really want?

Figure 1.1: A basic 7-Star Praying Mantis form.

You needn't reject that kind of thing altogether. I'm trying to show how to infuse those routines with an internal charge. Only then do they become supernaturally interesting and pleasurable. Lacking the energetic engagement, they're just somewhat lame floor gymnastics. Many people, even teachers, drill for decades on this stuff without ever experiencing the ultimate high it can bring.

To get there, you cannot *begin* with things like this Mantis form. It's guaranteed to degenerate into ordinary athletics. But if you work from the other end, putting the internal energy front and center, with practices that seem unglamorous and unathletic, then someday you can *return* to those livelier practices and meet them again, as though for the first time. Only then do they suddenly become supremely interesting, as you work on maintaining your whole-body 'charge' and on keeping your hands 'painted' with internal energy through the full set of vigorous athletics. I'll cover those things in this book. Then the traditional forms become a fascinating self-challenge game, more intriguing than any video play: *How long, and through what types of movement, can I maintain the charge unbroken?*

So there's nothing wrong with this Mantis set, per se. But there's a time and a place for everything. Later in this book I'll discuss how to integrate your newly found internal charge with your pre-existing athletic training. I'll return to that, but now I'll just say it's sad that so many students never experience what I'm talking about, just because they cannot stomach (literally!) the idea of relaxation and softness. They have some kind of mental or emotional block that prevents them from accessing it. Though everybody tries to put lipstick on the tension pig with words like *ligaments, fascia, tensegrity...* that verbiage just lets you lie to yourself about your tension. With all my stuff, there is no compromise on the requirement for actual relaxation – no physical tension beyond the minimum needed to create or maintain visible, yet empty, shape. Only that can lead the beginner toward 'mind boxing'.

I use the acronym MERGE, defined as follows:

Mind + *Extension* + *Relaxation* + *Grounding* = Energy

The first four letters are the essential ingredients of cultivating the last letter: E for energy. Most martial arts sets have you working excessively with Extension and forget everything else. I will show you practices that optimize all four ingredients. Mind you, this isn't a book purporting to scientifically prove the existence of *qi*. Those so-called 'bio-energy' or 'bio-electric' laboratory studies are unbearably boring, and probably completely misguided. Not to mention useless for your personal training. If you need a white coat to tell you what's real, look elsewhere. This book is for your operational experience, nothing more.

And as for *repetition*? Well, a turning screw, when viewed straight on, appears as pointlessly repetitive circular motion. But that's a limitation of the viewer's angle and ignorance. In reality, each turn of the screw is accomplishing deep work in an invisible dimension. That's what I aim for with the drills and teachings in this book.

Chapter 2

GUT FORCE MINING

Overview

The *niwan* point (mid-brain) is the ultimate fuel source and gas tank for the internal energy. The *tanden* (Chinese: 丹田 *dantian*), associated with the lower abdomen, can be thought of as the carburetor, where the fuel is activated, mixed and primed for conversion to functional power, which you can subsequently apply to martial arts. healing, and graphical productions such as calligraphy and painting.

carburetor : *a device for mixing vaporized fuel with air to produce a combustible or explosive mixture, as for an internal-combustion engine.*

The tradition of the *tanden* as a power source has always been the bedrock of internal teachings. Here's a typical formulation of the traditional concept, from the Xingyiquan classic writings:

必於臨敵挫陣之際常若有一團氣力堅凝於腹臍之間倏然自腰而背而項直貫於頂當時眼作先鋒以觀之心作元師以謀之

When attempting to overcome an enemy, you must continuously feel something like a sphere of massed power in your abdomen between your guts and navel. The energy then shoots up from your pelvis and sacrum, blasts along your spine and completely suffuses your head. This activates your eyes for observation, like scouts, and inspires your mind like a commander with a perfect tactical plan.

That summary describes the gist of the situation:

1. Power originating from lower body
2. Surging up along the back
3. Suffusing the head

The ARC as I've described it in other books includes all that. However, there's more to be said. That traditional account requires clarification, expansion, and additional refinement.

Let's dig into this thing about '*power originating from the lower body*'. The traditional account above begins with the hips and belly. The kidneys are also sometimes cited as power emitting organs. Those kinds of things are emphasized by many authors, without much mention of the legs and feet. For example, a contemporary account, written by a student of an established Tai Chi teacher, runs as follows:

> *One thing that is important to note is that* [my teacher's] *power doesn't come from the feet. He can convincingly demonstrate issuing while sitting down with his feet off the floor. It is all about expansion from the center.*

I am sympathetic with this account, and I understand that perception. It really feels that way in the moment of experience. However, from an analytical point of view, this is wrong. I could cite the Tai Chi classics here and shut down the whole discussion with this:

其根在腳,
Its origin in feet,

發於腿，
emitting in legs,
主宰於腰，
directed at waist,
形於手指。
forming in fingers.
由腳而腿而腰，
From feet then legs then waist,
總須完整一氣。
all must completely integrate one energy.

I'm giving a clunky, word-by-word, literal translation of those critical lines, to leave no room and no excuse for misunderstanding or ignorance. But legalistically citing this absolute authority is taking the easy way out. I want you to understand what these Classic writings, and my own books, are talking about at a deeper level.

I said it's wrong. But - if somebody is sitting down, with his/her feet off the floor, how can feet and legs be the origin of power in Tai Chi deployment? Yet in fact they are. As I discussed at length in my book *The Aiki Singularity*, anything can be your physical foundation. When you've understood the principle, your shins (*seiza*), your knees, or your butt (sitting in chair) – all can serve the function as your *physical* and *visible* mechanical foundation. But the feet and legs are also the *energetic* foundation, so their physical configuration actually doesn't matter much. They feed the power into your upper body *no matter how they're physically situated.*

That's why there are many demonstrations of seated push hands, and also the *seiza* version of Sagawa Yukiyoshi's *aiki-age*, etc. – all without standing on the feet. Those demonstrations don't mean that your lower body no longer has an energetic role in the ARC. But because Tai Chi training begins by standing up, it's natural to focus the discussion on the feet and legs as the normal learning foundation, both physical and energetic. If you're surprised that a Tai Chi master can still function with his "feet off the floor", or if you think that means the feet and legs are bypassed in energetic function, then you're still far from understanding Tai Chi.

Feet on or off the floor is a mechanical configuration. But real Tai Chi is an energy art. This confusion arises because the feet and legs also have an *energetic* role that is not the same as a mechanical function. *It's something different.* No matter how much I try to hammer that point in, it never seems to stick. People insist on mechanical, structural, and athletic interpretations. In real Tai Chi the feet do not function primarily as mechanical levers for the power (that would be ordinary physical stuff). They have a much more crucial role as amplifiers and relays for the internal force. That's what the R (Rebound) of the ARC is all about. But if you've never felt that in yourself, all you can do is describe the superficial visible shape.

The R in ARC stands for Rebound from below. In an ultimate spiritual sense, the internal energy is sourced from the brain center point (*niwan*) which is our body's main connection to the spirit energy source. However, for practical cultivation and deployment, the flow begins with the *tanden.* From there, contrary to the student's observations above, the power slams *downward*, then rebounds *upward* through the feet and legs once again, refills the 'center' (*tanden*) and is further boosted there, before surging through the upper body, eventually hitting hands for the Catch. This process has many details, but that's the essential ARC.

It is understandable why both the classical Xingyiquan overview above, and the student's comments about his teacher, ignore the role of feet and legs (thus deleting the R of the ARC). If you don't have personal experience with it, you won't understand that it's happening at all. It will seem that the power 'issues from the center". In fact, when working with a real master, it *should* seem to issue from the center.

Think of the 'look and feel' of computer mouse operation vs. its reality. The look and feel of it is a continuous glide of a unitary graphical object (the mouse pointer icon) across a static field (the graphic screen background). You don't perceive, and you don't think about, the reality of the operation. In fact, a complex mathematical transform is being continuously calculated, switching pixels on and off across the screen areas within an internal mathematical representation of the mouse unit's trajectory under your hand. There is no actual mouse pointer, in fact nothing other than your hand is actually 'moving'. It's all just pixel bits being turned off and on, which gives us a strong intuition of physically connected fluid movement. It's like an (imaginary) basketball player who dribbles so fast the ball never seems to leave his hands at all. Perception isn't always reality.

The perception of internal energy is strangely analogous. When the energy is in deployment mode, it's operating so fast that this foot-and-leg segment of the ARC, the Rebound, will be *perceived* as a single, solid, lower-body unit of stationary power, centered in the *tanden* and seeming to issue from there. When you slow things down in cultivation mode, working on yourself solo, you'll realize that the ARC is always operating – the Tai Chi Classics are technically correct though they seem intuitively 'wrong' in terms of user experience. However, if you haven't yet sparked the ARC in yourself, it's an easy mistake to make.

Furthermore, at a more advanced level, it's possible to train a process I call 'Sealing the ARC', which further tightens the lower body power unit, and integrates it with the upper body, to the point that, for all intents and purposes, the entire ARC with all its segments becomes a single solid-state full-body phenomenon. That's the main outcome of working the methods in this book. I'll be unpacking it further as we go. For now, the point to remember is that the power is always launching from the *energetic foundation* which for Tai Chi is the feet and legs. But once you seal the ARC, which connects the origin (*tanden*) and terminus (hands) down your front, it will seem to others that power issues directly from your center.

Now let's get back to the *tanden* per se, because the Rebound energy starts with Activation from there. In my books so far, I've skimmed over the training aspects of *tanden* cultivation too lightly. When it comes to priming and pumping the *tanden*, specifying how to really work it, more can be said. In my brief, informal video demonstration showing the Tai Chi belly-tossing of a rock (丹田彈抖功), which I will cover in detail later in this chapter, I said the following:

> *This demonstration shows the coordinated hard wave, which is the beginner level of Tai Chi energy. I explained the hard wave in my book* Juice. *This stunt shows an internal attribute, but it's the closest to the physical. It's not evidence of profound Tai Chi skill. The ability emerges naturally from practicing any internal method. Obviously it's not a combative skill. But any professional instructor of any internal martial art - Tai Chi, Xingyi, Bagua, Yiquan, anything ... Liuhebafa... they all can do this. But they don't show it often. Why not? First, it isn't much use in combatives. Second, it isn't a very dignified position, or action to perform, is it?*

I posted that video in response to a trolling challenge. But I learned something from the responses. This stone-tossing stunt itself may not be of compelling interest. But people are intensely curious about *tanden* training and conditioning. I've talked about amazing energy effects in my books. But I've started to realize that few students are relaxed and aware enough, in their *tanden*, to reach all the good stuff. That's my fault. I have assumed that because I personally have felt and worked with the *tanden* energy tangibly, from a fairly early stage, all others must be the same.

When it comes to the *tanden* I've mostly just said: '*activate it*'. Then I've sailed straight on to the rest of the ARC model. So even though the 'A' of the ARC stands for 'Accumulate in *tanden*', that step hasn't been as easy or obvious as I'd assumed. Teachers love to say things like 'move from the *tanden*'. But in practice most so-called 'movement from the *tanden*' is only the usual MEAT (Mechanically Engaged Application of Tension). I'm going to fix that here and now by stepping you through a detailed training protocol that will:

(a) get you feeling the (Accumulate) *tanden* energy like never before; and
(b) supercharge the two later stages (Rebound and Catch)

I call this the Tanden Activation Protocol (TAP). It offers a hyper-amplification of your return-on-practice investment. It will pay off big, no matter what style of internal martial arts you practice.

Readers who have deep backgrounds in breathwork, yoga, or *neidan* systems will feel some familiarity. I'm taking this *tanden* work deeper into a kind of semi-physical breathwork than I usually do. Naturally, there are points where all systems converge. That's because the basic ingredients are limited (abdomen, lungs, body, mind). But here you will find unique refinements and points of emphasis, strung together along a baseline of radical simplicity. Your experience of these 'perpendicular' protocols will thus be more interesting and productive, or least fresher, than much of what you may have worked on in the past. But before I get to the full TAP, I need to cover some essentials.

The Hard Wave

First you need to taste the 'hard wave'. This isn't 'hard' in the sense of ordinary athletic martial arts training. It's a completely different concept. At the risk of more repetition, I need to review this. Because, in my years of running seminars and private teaching since the appearance of *Juice*, I've found there is little basic awareness of this attribute, much less any deep understanding. Not to mention a paucity of actual experience. I blame myself for that. I haven't gone into the training specifics deeply enough. So bear with me while I rewind back to one of the first drills and illustrations in *Juice*.

Figure 2.1: Your first taste of the 'hard wave'

This tabletop hand play isn't really a work-a-day drill. It's more just a proof-of-concept, or teaser, for the hard wave concept. However, it has everything needed to get you some hard wave experience.

You rest your forearm perpendicular to the table, and extend your fingers. As they're extending, try to relax them (even though that may sound contradictory). We have here everything we need. The Mind, Extension, Relaxation and Grounding from the fundamental MERGE concept I mentioned earlier are all present in one forearm drill. You'll be keeping your forearm steady and unmoving throughout. As you slowly wave your hand backwards and forward, bending at the wrist, you lightly concentrate on extending while relaxing. Eventually, you'll feel a vibration running from your foundation (elbow) through the forearm, wrist, hand, and out your fingers. It's clear and obvious and entirely unmistakable once you experience it. But if we stop the discussion here, the deeper point of it all may not be clear.

This is the easiest way to have your first experience of the hard wave. The more you play with it, the more interesting features you'll notice. Pay attention to the vibratory frequency. Though this particular hard wave drill is not explicitly tied to breath, you will realize at some point that the little bumps are happening at about 3 or 4 per breath action (a single inhale or single exhale). That's an almost invariant feature of the hard wave across all shapes and sizes of people. In this particular drill, the vibrations are experienced most sharply and directly in the working forearm and hand. But the waves are eventually mirrored in your *tanden*, and finally extend throughout your body - even these forearm-triggered waves. The same whole body engagement will happen with the *tanden*-centric hard waves introduced in this section.

I use the term 'hard wave' only to set up a contrast with the subsequent higher state of energy, which I call the 'soft wave'. The soft wave feels radically different, but it derives from assembling and accelerating the hard wave. But the terminology is weird, because the so-called 'hard wave' isn't really hard. It's not like any kind of tension or muscle. Its impact within your body is soft. But the word 'hard' is intended, first, to contrast with the follow-on 'soft' mode, and, second, to emphasize how clear, crisp and sharp the energy bumps feel.

The hard wave is a *training* tool. It isn't an end in itself. It has no *direct* function in fighting or healing. As a state or experience, it's interesting but in no way comparable to gonzo blowout coolness of the higher energetic states. And after all, you can't go around visibly vibrating all day either.

But the hard wave *is* the essential link between the physical and the energetic. It's a hybrid phenomena that bridges the chasm. Many teachers and books will assert that *breath* is the bridge between the gross physical and the energetic/spiritual realms. But that's not quite right. Breath is *physical*, plain and simple. It's a mechanical and physiological process of the body. In reality, your breath is the pylon or support pillar on the physical side, anchoring the hard wave. The hard wave is the bridge. The hard wave fastens to the breath on one side, and merges into the truly energetic *soft wave* on the other side. When you're able to generate and control the hard wave, you'll then quickly learn to transition it to the *soft wave*, which is like a powerful full-body 'wash' effect.

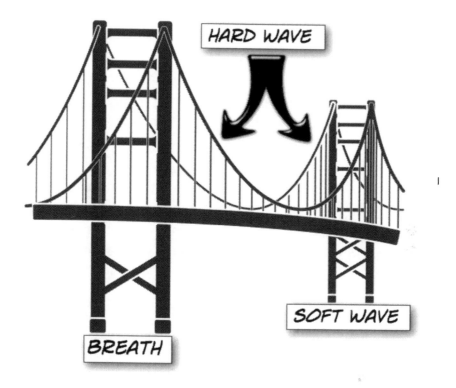

Figure 2.2: The hard wave is the bridge between the physical (breath) and the energetic (soft wave).

The hard wave is like the warmup phase of a propeller plane on the tarmac. When untrained people are breathing in daily life (including athletic activity), the energy is not actively engaged. This corresponds to a stopped airplane propeller. The blades are all visible because they are inactive, stopped and dead. As the engines warmup, the propeller begins to move. The rotations are slow and regular and each individual blade remains distinctly visible. The soft wave is when the engines rev up immediately prior to takeoff. The blades spin so fast and their frequency is so high that they all seem to merge and are no longer separately visible. You can only feel a highly energetic hum, vibration, or shimmer in the area where they're spinning. The situation with the three states: ordinary breathing, hard wave, soft wave, is analogous. Once you can trigger and control the hard wave, you can speed it up and transition it to a wash of soft energy, radiating through your body at the command of your mind.

Figure 2.3: Propeller warm-up process is analogous to the states: breath, hard wave, and soft wave.

Continuing with the hand drill as a jumping-off place, notice its vertical orientation. That is, the wave propagates vertically through the upright forearm, from foundation at elbow to extension at fingers. The wave axis is aligned to the physical instrument. In the Tanden Activation Protocol, we'll work on this same hard wave. But it will be realigned to run perpendicular to the instrument (your body). Before that, you must be able to locate and feel directly into your *tanden* point.

Feeling the Tanden Spot

Traditional acupuncture charts show your body bristling with points like a de-quilled porcupine. But for energy training, that's too much of a good thing. You only need a few critical points for non-medical internal energy training. Over-focus on the minutiae of point proliferation will only distract you and tense you up. However, at certain stages, under-standing a few essential points is useful. One of those is the *tanden* (丹田) generally said to be in the lower abdomen. I use the word *tanden* because it rolls off the tongue more easily than the Chinese term *dantian*, but they are the same Chinese characters. It's all the same thing. Regardless of the terminology, it needs to be unpacked in a unique understanding that I'll show you here.

The *tanden* is highlighted throughout the internal literature. But a lot of people have no idea what the fuss is about. They never feel anything special there and don't see what special energy could be derived from it (apart from maybe some kind of physical torque). Sometimes that lack of experience leads to total denial of the traditional Asian view of internal energy. Consider this opinion, from somebody who could have gone a lot deeper:

> So I see the concept of ki *and* chi *as an incredible impediment to learning and I see people in classes, Aikido and Kung Fu and what-ever, and it's just a struggle. They can never get it. They never get it because the idea of* chi *or* ki *is preposterous. How can you get it if it's a point in your stomach? What would you do with such a point? What can you do with it? What change will it make to you? Now,*

it sounds like a mysterious kind of super power that you get from somewhere in the point in your stomach, and that point described properly, is the duodenum lying there and is literally full of shit.
   - Feldenkrais

People who want to deny the reality of internal energy still hope to keep some coherence with the thousand-year tradition of this area's energy significance. So they usually pitch a re-interpretation of the *tanden* thing as a physical property, a way of moving or using your muscles for maximal mechanical efficacy:

It has to do with the full organization of your body, you can see it in whatever you do. You actually get chi *through using the pelvis and the lower abdominal muscles, the strong muscles of the body as a unit concentrated from where all push or pull is issued. The improvement in your movement that you get moving the head free so that the pelvis can produce the necessary power, that's ki. How do you 'send energy' here or there? Show me any instance where you can send energy anywhere.*
   - Feldenkrais

What can you do with such a point...? If you've never been exposed to the real internal training, the above conclusions are reasonable. But for Feldenkrais, it was a case of insufficient experience. There really is an internal energy. It has some correlation to the physical. But it differs so greatly from the ordinary understanding and methods of physical power that we might as well call it non-physical.

Normally the *tanden* is described as a single smallish point. It's usually emphasized that this is *inside* the abdomen. It's supposed to be a certain number of inches down from the navel and another few inches straight inside. This is not totally wrong. But it's not as useful in practical training for internal energy activation as the breakdown I'll now provide.

The traditional description is mashing together two things that are related but distinct. One thing you need is a specific mental hook to begin your mental engagement with the *tanden*. Without that you can't train it. This is the problem that many people have written to me about: '*I can't feel anything special there.*' The other aspect is understanding the broader zone (of your energy body) which that training point activates.

So, think of two distinct but related components. The first is like a medium-size ball in the lower abdomen. Every body differs, but imagine a volleyball which comfortably fills the interior of the space defined by the hips on the sides and the navel and sacrum back-to-front. This is the *tanden* as a zone. It's a broad area larger than a single point. This concept overlaps with the traditional Japanese *hara*, or physical body centroid. In the illustration, you can see a large ball representing the *hara*, and I'll call that the T-Ball – the *tanden* as a ball. This is useful but it's too general as a beginner's training concept. Everybody knows the word *hara* and has heard the general idea. But it's rare to find somebody who feels the power for real.

To kick start operations in the most tangible way, you'll need a second, more refined focus point. The formula "*x fingers down from navel and y fingers inward*" is not optimal for working this stuff. Apart from medical pain, most people simply can't feel much inside themselves. Everybody is so tense and insensitive. So we'll imagine a point location that's much easier to relate to and which drills a path into the larger *hara* space.

The outer front surface of your belly corresponds to the outer circumference of the T-Ball sphere. The black circle in the center of the T-Ball illustration represents your navel. The navel is familiar and tangible on the *outer* surface of the belly. Now we can use a part of the traditional locator formula. A few finger-widths down from the navel – but *remaining on the surface* - there's a place, just below the navel, where regardless of how fat or fit you may be, the belly protuberance reaches a maximum and crests. Below that point, it begins curving back down and inward to the pubic bone.

That cresting point, right on the skin surface, is your T-Spot. This differs from the traditional formula, because we're not going *inside* the belly yet. We're going to work with this surface point as the gateway to your first tangible *tanden* experience.

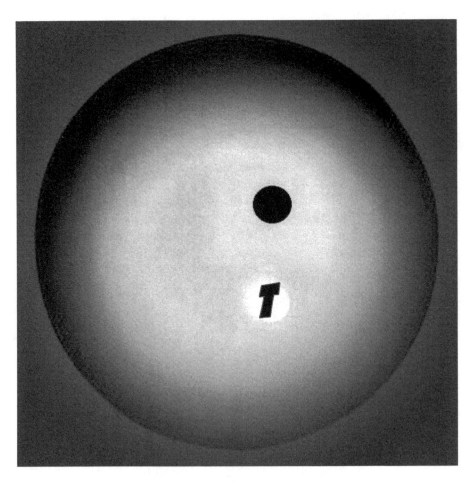

Figure 2.4: The large sphere represents the T-Ball, which entirely fills your lower abdomen. The black point is the navel. The bright point beneath is the T-Spot.

There's a practical way to work this point. I received this teaching for getting started with *tanden* conditioning from my traditional Xingyi-quan teacher, along with a lot of other augmentations and backdoor codes into the real internal energy. It took me a few decades to understand and unravel it all though. I have given this drill out freely in a video clip on my YouTube channel. I also touched on this briefly in one of my other books, but I soft-pedaled it so much that I doubt anybody noticed. So emphasizing it more now.

In training, you should be able to instantly engage your T-Spot. When you're able to do that, you can 'charge' up a stream of ARC power instantaneously. But you need familiarity with the feel of it. To carve the awareness of this point into my neural circuits, my teacher had me stand in a classical Xingyi training pose – but with a special added twist.

A long, wooden pole will be lightly set or pressed at the surface of your *tanden* – the T-Spot. Your job is to use minimal movements of your body and T-Ball to move your T-Spot *away* from the pole tip – *without* letting the pole drop. Impossible? That's the whole point. Work at the razor's edge of that contradiction, that's where the power originates.

Beginning with a certain Xingyi stance (I'll get into whether that's strictly necessary down below), the following checklist applies:

- Far end of pole angled down. braced against wall or object
- Other end placed lightly and precisely on your T-Spot
- Pressed gently *against* T-Spot, not resting on top of belly curve
- Draw away from the pole – but don't let it slip down at all
- After a few minutes, repeat on the opposite side

Figure 2.5: Move your T-Spot away from the pole tip, but don't let the pole slip down even a fraction of an inch. It's a contradiction - deal with it.

This work will kick start your awareness of the exact location and feeling of the T-Spot, which is the gateway to all *tanden* training. Don't worry that it targets a surface point. The traditional formula emphasizes the more interior aspect of the *tanden*. But if you can't feel anything you can't feed anything. This drill radically sensitizes you to the reality of the *tanden*.

There are two practical issues with this drill. First is the stance. The stance shown is the classical static posture of Xingyiquan called *santishi*. I've covered that exhaustively in many other books and videos. But I don't want accusations of up-selling or cross-marketing and all that. It's not essential to practice this using only that one stance. That's just how it was taught to me.

You'll get equal results from using any other stance. For example, if you know Tai Chi, you could substitute the Raise Hands pose (illustrated in the next chapter) instead of *santishi*. If you don't know any stance at all, just stand facing the wall with your feet parallel and shoulder-width apart. Place the pole as directed and work it from there. Even this minimal version will radically sensitize you to your T-Spot, and eventually extend to the T-Ball.

The pole is the other problem. But it's not necessary always to have a pole handy, every day, wherever you go. Work with the pole as often as possible. But if you can do this drill using the pole for a few days running, the necessary sensation will be etched into your mind. You can then trigger a virtual version of the T-Spot engagement every day, in any stance, wherever you are, even without a pole. Once you've tasted that, it stays with you. It's like the difference on a web page between simple, flat text vs. hyperlinked text. The hypertext looks and feels different to your mouse, eyes and mind than the plaintext. Even if you don't actually click the link, you're aware of the difference. This drill permanently hyperlinks your T-Spot so that it feels different.

But even this T-Spot pole work is only *preparatory*. Do it regularly but forget about it, if that makes sense. It will perform its magical enablement softly, behind the scenes, helping to boost and amplify the further *tanden* work coming up in this chapter and the next.

Posture, Principles, and Practice

Next, we're going to rotate the wave axis, relative to its physical foundation. To perpendicularize it, we'll work from the classical yoga corpse pose – *shavasana*. We're using something that looks like yoga, and we begin with some yoga-sounding prep work. But the goal here is – as always – to develop the internal non-physical energy of classical martial arts more deeply. We aren't doing this for stress reduction or spiritual integration or any of the other yoga clichés.

Here's the classical *shavasana* specification:

> *"Lying flat on the ground with the face upwards, in the manner of a dead body, is shavasana. It removes tiredness and enables the mind (and whole body) to relax."*
> - Hatha Yoga Pradipika

So relaxation is going to be key from the start. In this configuration, your body is horizontal. But we're going to run the hard wave energy perpendicularly (vertically) to the full body orientation.

Figure 2.6: Shavasana

Now, carefully extract your femoral hematopoietic marrow and wind it around the base of your *pingala nadi* three times, counter-clockwise ... wait! Just kidding. I know you'd like more mysterious Oriental bells and whistles on this stuff. But let's continue with the straight dope.

Breathing is going to be involved, but this isn't breathwork per se. Don't get into Ashtanga *ujjayi* breathing for this. You continue to breathe –

that's true of almost everything we do. But thinking of this primarily as a breathing protocol will limit your experience and understanding. I'll cover more on breath in the next section. For now, it's preferable to think of this as "relaxation and natural breath movement". That's the essence of Tai Chi itself. But normally when it comes to "movement" people are very arm-centric and stance-centric. We're going to apply the Tai Chi idea of relaxed, gentle movement, which is normally expressed with the arms (in upright vertical mode), to the lower belly, which will be horizontal. This is the foundation for working toward the internal hard wave, localized in your *tanden*.

Natural Perpendicular Protocol

Always begin the session with basic *shavasana*. Lie there and relax, mentally check your state, lightly run over your body from feet to head with your mind. Here's where I could make a huge deal out of 'progressive relaxation' (checking and removing tension from each body part in turn). Some bodywork books would turn that into a whole chapter or more. But you get the idea. It's simple enough. Take a minute for that when you first lie down.

Hard Wave Perpendicular Protocol

Now it's time to consciously generate and experience the hard wave in this perpendicular orientation. If you were able to experience the hard wave with the hand drill, then you have a head start on catching the first faint sensations. Though initially faint, don't give up. If you follow the entire protocol of this chapter consistently for a few weeks, and cultivate the power through technique drills (to be discussed in later chapters), you'll be totally blown away by the experience.

As you lie there, relaxed, place your mind gently into your mid and lower abdomen. Breathe fully, but for now keep a natural rhythm and expansion/contraction. Don't shape any particular motion yet, just be aware of the slight expansion of your lower abdomen on the inhale, slight subsidence on the exhale. Each 'breath action' (a single inhale or a single exhale) should take you about one natural second, give or take. Go slow but not unnaturally so. Feel your mind and body deeply with each breath without trying to goose or game any special effects for now.

There's to be no forcing. For now, don't sauce it up with any special breathing technique. If you rush forward to exotic breathing techniques you'll overlook the natural power of these practices – which is *beyond the physical*. But it isn't 'psychological' or 'spiritual' either. It's *energetic* and completely mind-blowing in and of itself.

At first you'll probably only be able to detect the mild physical tissue expansion and subsidence in each breath cycle (single inhale/exhale pair). To notice the hard wave vibrations, you need to inject your mind more deeply into your entire lower abdominal and pelvic area.

Imagine a rubber ball rolling down a short (4- or 5-step) stairway. One complete run of the ball from top to bottom will correspond to the idea of one full 'breath action' (a single inhale or a single exhale). Imagine how the ball 'feels' as it rolls down. It's experiencing a gentle thump on each drop from one step to the next. Those three or four bumps correspond to the several whumps of the hard wave inside your lower abdomen, as you work a single breath action. (Balls don't normally roll *up* staircases with the same natural ease as going down, but the basic metaphor should put across the idea - it applies to *both* inhale and exhale actions.)

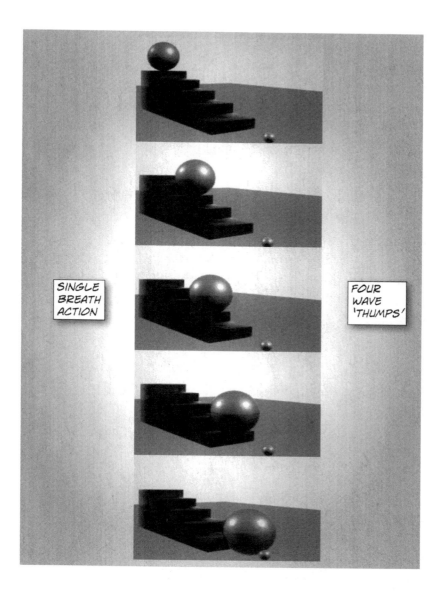

Figure 2.7: Each bump down a step represents a thump of the hard wave during a single breath action.

BUBBLE Breathing Perpendicular Protocol

The basic Hard Wave Perpendicular Protocol above is a step beyond the Natural Protocol, but so far it's only awareness and sensing, not a physical engagement of direct control. In this next protocol, you begin a very gentle and sensitive controlling function. It may seem that we are moving toward garden-variety forced 'belly breathing'. But keep reading, it isn't quite the normal thing.

There are at least a hundred versions of "belly breathing". I co-wrote a popular breathing book that includes a lot of related material. And I've done intensive training in the root method of all breathwork systems – the classical Indian *pranayama* protocols. I learned those via traditional Ashtanga Yoga (Shri K. Pattabhi Jois method). That includes *kriya nauli,* and a lot of other breath stuff. I've also done intensive training in the Chinese energy-breath linkage methods, such as Taoist alchemical regimens.

But rather than belly breathing, deep breathing, *pranayama*, *nauli*, reverse breathing, breath of fire, or any of those common forced-breath regimens, I'll introduce my own term: BUBBLE (Ballooning Undulatory Belly Ball Lifting Expansion). Some people froth rabidly at the mouth whenever they see an acronym, so if you're one of those pedants, forget it's an acronym and treat it as a plain word, like LASER, RADAR or SCUBA - which are also acronyms. The main difference between belly breathing and BUBBLE breathing is the slow, relaxed meditative expansion of the latter. When you do Tai Chi, you should (eventually) feel the various waves, currents and ripples through your *limbs*. With the TAP and BUBBLE breathing you'll feel these energies directly inside your *tanden*. For many students that will be a first. It's like doing energy-centric Tai Chi with your diaphragm instead of your arms and legs.

The mechanics are straightforward. As you lie there, inhale through either mouth alone or both mouth and nose together. Allow that to happen naturally – don't force the timing or amplitude of it in the beginning.

As you inhale, put your mind into your lower belly and, very gently and calmly, while allowing the air to flow into yourself, allow your lower belly to expand upward and outward. Feel the action centered from, or peaking at, the T-Spot explained earlier. But now, the entire surface of the lower abdomen (front of T-Ball) is also involved in the expansion. It should be a very distinctive feeling, somehow a sensation of opening – not tensing or jamming in any way. Feel the hard wave thumps as you expand. Now as you exhale through your nose, or nose and mouth together (equally), allow your belly to subside back down. Feel the hard wave thumps as it sinks. Repeat.

Figure 2.8: The *tanden* ball (T-Ball) is gently expanded and lifted like a balloon, then subsides. Feel the hard waves throughout.

Now I hear your mental screech: *"Hey! That's nothing but run-of-the-mill belly breathing!"* Well... yes and no. If you've heard of "belly breathing" (available as a space-filler article in about every other issue of every martial arts, yoga, or general health magazine ever published), you know it's a staple thing when they need a few more lines of "article" to balance the ad pages. Belly breathing is constantly touted everywhere as a stress reducer, an anger management tool, and a cheesy peace-of-mind hack. What I'm showing you in this section has some commonality with that. But the purposes and results of this work (and most of the details) differ substantially from what you've seen in your supermarket checkout reading.

The hard wave is the entire point of all these Protocols. The cheesy 'health mag' version of deep breathing, as well as the sophisticated routines of *pranayama* in Ashtanga yoga, all involve a degree of force that will block your hard wave. So don't turn this into a physical forcing regimen like the others. BUBBLE breathing uses the same principles as Tai Chi overall. No matter how ordinary these physical actions may appear, the underlying substance and result of these Protocols has almost nothing in common with yoga or fitness or stress reduction breath methods. This isn't a 'breath method' at all. It's a way of using mental awareness to mine the energetic potential of gentle and relaxed physical gestures. In that way, it's the same as Tai Chi overall.

It perplexes me how hard this concept is for most people to take seriously. People brush past it as a checklist thing. I know I'm repeating myself, but at least you're getting off easier than I have, in that my Tai Chi teacher has probably told me to relax over 10,000 times (very much as the great Yang Chengfu repeated to his students, by all reports).

Weighted Perpendicular Protocol

In the weighted Protocol, we put a small object on the *tanden* spot (as identified earlier). Don't go crazy with this! Especially at the beginning it needs to be a small, light object. A flattish rock weighing 8 to 16 ounces or so is an ideal starter weight. The purpose of this is *not* to develop your muscles or tone your abs. If that's your interest, you should be doing crunches on the ab machine. We're using the weight because having a material object there assists in focusing your *mind* on the lower abdomen. Having some light and gentle resistance to the relaxed, expansive movements of the BUBBLE breathing will tease out not only where your lower abdomen is still tense, but other areas of tension in your hips, lower back, pelvis and thighs. Gently use your lower abdomen to raise the weight with each inhale, then let it slowly subside with each exhale. Try to feel the hard waves while doing so.

As you do that, try your best to feel into your pelvis, especially where it contacts the floor. Have you established and maintained a good *foundation*? The foundation concept in this Perpendicular work is identical to the foundation at the elbow in the hand waving drill. It's the same role your feet play in ordinary Tai Chi. You'll find yourself unconsciously trying to 'assist' the lift with your hips, lower back, or pelvis. In normal athletics, this kind of entrainment may be a good thing, an actual skill. Here though – *not so much*. I'll get into a Tai Chi version of entrainment in a later section. For now, try to relax everything and isolate the gently expansive lift of the object with your abdominal surface alone – your T-Ball under your T-Spot, and the T-Spot directly supporting the object.

When you're comfortable with the object on your T-Spot, you can learn to feel the hard waves more easily as follows. Normally your arms are relaxed along your sides in *shavasana*. As a variation for this weighted work, you can gently place your fingers on top of the weight object, near the edges. Keep your elbows relaxed on the floor as you do this. It's only a finger thing. Put no more than 4 ounces of continuous finger pressure on the object as you continue the BUBBLE expansion and deflation. The very slight resistance of your fingers, or really just the awareness of your fingers, will help to trigger and intensify the hard waves. After 5 or so

BUBBLE breaths with finger pressure, return your hands to your sides and continue with normal BUBBLE work. You will feel even more aware of the object and your T-Spot and T-Ball than before.

Advanced Yogic Protocol

One of the strongest and clearest methods for feeling the hard wave in the gut is the yoga pose called *baddha padmasana,* or 'Bound Lotus'. This is probably the most effective concentrator of the hard wave in the gut, gently riding on your breath. However, while the energetic part is the same simple, strain-free procedure already explained for Perpendicular mode, the physical mechanics of Bound Lotus may be challenging for some people. If you have any doubt about your ability to safely and comfortably execute this pose, don't attempt it. Better safe than sorry. The other exercises will cumulatively offer the same effects.

If you are able to handle it safely and comfortably, then get into the pose. Relax and calm your mind. Then gently focus on the lower abdominal region, as before. You will find that this pose helps you mentally spotlight that precise region and the binding helps to focus the power like a lens. Gently expand your lower abdomen, like a small ball, on the inhale, then allow it to gently subside on the exhale. With each such breath action, you will eventually come to experience the 3 or 4 *'separate yet linked'* shock waves of the hard wave effect, propagating from the *tanden* region. You can either mentally restrict the pulses to your abdominal region, or you can experiment with allowing them to ripple through your entire body. The tight physical integration of your body in this pose helps to create a single 'medium' for the maximal outward rippling of the wave from your abdomen.

Once you get the hard wave going, concentrate on the exact point where your fingers are holding your feet. This 'binding' instantly ignites and amplifies the wave even further. In this pose and practice, more than any other, you'll feel your entire body becoming a single, undifferentiated medium for the unimpeded hard resonance. There won't be any dead zones or dangling loose ends when you rock the hard wave in lotus pose.

Don't go hog-wild with it. You can perform 20 to 30 breath cycles in a session. But over time, doing this pose with the hard wave awareness will amp your gut power by a big multiplier (substantial carry over to forms and martial arts training). Thousands of yoga people do this pose every day, with standard Ashtanga *ujyayyi* breathing, but they don't pick up on the deeper carryover effect because they're working for different goals.

Figure 2.9: Baddha Padmasana (Bound Lotus).

Gut-Toss Protocol

Finally we hit the money shot: the *gut-toss demonstration*. Well-known masters of Chen Style Tai Chi (such as Wang Zhanjun) have appeared on national Chinese television, lying supine and launching a rock or metal disc from their bellies, tossing it a few feet of distance. What is the relation, if any, of those kinds of crowd-pleasing feats to the *tanden* training I've been covering in this chapter? Are these stunts evidence of advanced internal power? Does the stunt have some kind of deeper value to advance the broader training goals of Tai Chi?

Warning: this section is going to be kind of confusing. I'm going to tell you:

- That this is a mere *stunt* – yet it has hidden *training* potential.
- That any *mediocre* Tai Chi student can do it – yet it's *harder* than it looks.
- That it emerges *naturally* and organically – yet there's a *method* to it.
- That it's mainly *internal* – yet I'll give you some *physical* pointers.
- That it has nothing to do with real Tai Chi as a *skill* – yet it relies on and develops profound Tai Chi *attributes*.

Confusing? You bet. But if you don't want to wade through all the verbiage, skip straight down to the training protocol.

The *attributes* that are used for the gut-tossing feat are closely related to the foundations of genuine Tai Chi development (those gut-tossing masters are for real). On the other hand, you can develop the basic internal attributes in many other ways, and use them for many other purposes, without ever getting near the gut-toss, neither for training nor validation.

Furthermore, there's a danger in this stunt. Not a physical hazard. But it's overly dramatic quality may lead to privileging something visible and (quasi) physical over the true internal experience - as we humans are apt to do. This is the same temptation that leads people to adulate push-hands champions who are simply skilled wrestling athletes (this applies to some, not all, push hands champs). I discourage any student from working on this stunt *as a goal in itself.* At best it's nothing but a distraction, and at worst it will permanently warp the student's perception of the real value and goals of internal training. The gut-toss stunt has as much relation to either the combatives or energetics of Tai Chi as sword-swallowing has to Olympic fencing. Yet even sword-swallowing has something to teach.

Figure 2.10: Does sword-swallowing carry over to Olympic fencing?

The gut-toss stunt is associated with Chen Style Tai Chi. While in my teens, I had an unplanned and unexpected chance to train that style on the side. This was decades before Chen Style Tai Chi rocketed to market dominance in the West. So I've known about this stunt for a long time. But I never took it seriously until I recently got an email challenging me to show it. So I did a performance video exhibiting a modest toss, which triggered a surprisingly enthusiastic response. That's why I'm covering it in this book. But you must conceptually separate the gut toss, as a performance goal, from the full TAP training program. The huge benefit of the TAP lies in another direction – to enhance your foundation for the higher internal energies, not to bounce rocks. But as one *part* of the TAP attribute program, the gut toss can have value. And based on the email response to my video, there's a fair amount of interest in learning something about the details of the gut toss.

In fact, if you've been working the TAP presented so far in this chapter, over a fair period of weeks or months, you already have the ability to do this stunt. Even without the TAP, just by virtue of practicing any internal art with proper attention to physical relaxation and sinking coupled with mental expansion and extension, some people will naturally develop the ability to do this. I once thought *every* Tai Chi or Qi Gong teacher could do it. But since my video has come out, I've had reports that this assumption isn't necessarily correct. It seems that the gut toss is somewhat more challenging, even for some experienced people, than I had realized.

Yet some people without *any* basic Tai Chi (or other internal systems) training will naturally have this ability. It's like the splits, as 'a physical feat with some mental engagement'. Some people undergo a rigorous and specific training regimen over a long time to get that ability. Others will drop into full splits within a few days of first trying it out. I am a 'natural' for both flexibility and the gut-toss stunt (but not for lots of other things). That's why it never occurred to me to cover the gut toss in my earlier books. But though from one angle it's a sideline party game, it can become a platform which deeply works your basic TAP attributes. We will approach it in that spirit.

FRONT SPLITS TYPE 1
AGE: 16
PRACTICE: SHAOLIN KUNGFU
VERSION: OPEN HIP
NAME: 劈叉

FRONT SPLITS TYPE 2
AGE: 60
PRACTICE: ASHTANGA YOGA
VERSION: CLOSED HIP
NAME: HANUMANASANA

Figure 2.11: Flexibility can be a natural attribute or trained.

The beauty of it is that by drilling the TAP as presented so far, you're set up to do the Gut Toss demo. It's just a (practical?) application of the relaxed BUBBLE shaping. As your experimental toss object, you can use a flattish rock of about 8 to 12 oz. weight or a flat, circular padlock. The padlock is good because it has pretty much radially uniform weight in a saucer-like shape.

Figure 2.12: This lock is an ideal object for gut toss experimentation.

You need to keep the following points foremost in your mind. The main thing is to relax. The first time you try this, there'll be an almost irresistible temptation to try to muscle the object up and out. That's totally wrong. If you persist in that you will never achieve this little feat. The gut toss requires a gentle and sensitive corralling of the normally time-spaced hard waves into a unitary harmonized gesture. *But physical exertion kills the hard wave energy.* That's the deeper Tai Chi lesson this stunt teaches you. Using muscle is a sign of purely external work, based on mechanical contraction, closure and cramping. The gut toss is exactly the *opposite* – it's a feat of relaxing, opening, and expanding. It is not so much power as it is sensitivity. That's what makes it a quasi-internal operation.

You may think this Chen Style stunt relies on muscular development in the abdomen. Maybe you think it results from exotic training like yoga *nauli* (abdominal muscle isolation). Or maybe you need sexy 6-pack abs? Not at all. If you think like that you'll never get it. My Tai Chi teacher always says, as we hold Zheng Style Tai Chi stances: "*Make your belly soft like a bag of water, not hard like a block of ice*". This is the meaning of the Tai Chi classic writing: '*belly thoroughly relaxed*' (腹鬆淨). Do the bellies in the graphic look more like '*bags of water*' or more like '*blocks of ice*'? You be the judge.

Figure 2.13: Abdominal development: yoga *nauli* (left), 6-pack abs (right). None of this matters for the gut toss.

Lie in *shavasana*, same as the TAP practice. Center your toss object directly on your T-Spot. Exhale gently but thoroughly. Now inhale and expand the lower belly. It's the BUBBLE shaping, just as you've done in the TAP training. This establishes a kind of support 'platform' for the toss object. Now, while gently *stilling* (not hard holding) your breath, allow the expanded belly to subside. As you subside and your belly lowers, don't release the 'platform' feeling completely. Try to maintain a kind of mental support for the object, and engagement with it. Really feel your object, be sensitive to its weight and position. When you've lowered enough to create suitable throwing range, quickly expand your belly again into exactly the same TAP dome shape - but for this work, do it rapidly.

Do *not* try to contract forcefully and muscle it. No matter how much effort you put into it, that kind of physical exertion will kill the throw. Just gently launch it 'upward'. Let the 'outward' aspect (down toward feet) take care of itself. Toss the object up with a mental feeling of expansion and opening. As you perform the tossing gesture, keep the rest of your body (head, neck, shoulders, arms hands, legs) as relaxed as possible.

The biggest confusion will come up in the area of breath. Obviously the setup phase must be an inhale, to build the little inner abdominal T-Ball supporting the object. You then allow the abdomen to subside in preparation for the throw, and that's where the breath management requires some subtlety and sensitivity.

Most people will assume, before trying it themselves, that a good toss must require a forceful exhalation. That's totally wrong. Remember this is a Tai Chi attribute practice, not Karate. A forceful exhale will drain all your throw power. You'll barely be able to jiggle the object on your belly.

In all my books, I've said: forget about your breath. Don't stop breathing (obviously!) but don't make a big thing out of it. Most especially, don't try to consciously coordinate breath to the Tai Chi gestures. That stiffens and deadens both mind and body. An example would be some teachers' insistence that an 'outgoing' movement like a push should be done with an exhale, and a gathering or contracting movement is to be done with an inhale. That's an extremely crude approach to Tai Chi.

This TAP work is horizontal Tai Chi. We are working toward Tai Chi attributes from within the Tai Chi concept space. Don't dump all that overboard just because you hope to show off a belly toss. And it won't work anyway. The setup for the toss does require an expansive BUBBLE inhale to create the platform. But for the toss itself you need to forget about your breath. Forgetting the breath isn't the same as holding your breath. Holding your breath requires firm closure of your mouth, uvular flap, and/or glottis, plus some abdominal rigidity. That's all wrong. What I mean by 'stilling' is to stay relaxed so the passage is left open. Your toss gesture can then naturally draw in a little air as you throw.

Basically it's the opposite of what most (even veteran Tai Chi people) would assume. Instead of a big, forceful exhale; the ideal breath of the toss gesture is a gentle, minimal, relaxed slight *inhale*. When you've really understood the gesture itself, the breath matters less and less. Later you'll be able to do it on a slight, gentle *exhale* just as well. Either way is fine, but it's easier to learn at first by stilling your breath or even allowing a minimal inhale. This work gives you deeper insight on one confusing line of the Tai Chi classic writings: "*concentration on the breath depletes power*" (有氣者無力). It's confusing because the character 'qi' (氣) can mean either real internal power or ordinary breath. In that line, it refers to breath. If you attempt the gut toss with a powerful breath action, you will never get it. In this way, the gut toss is identical to Tai Chi push hands principles.

There's another aspect to this, and again it helps us in exploring foundational Tai Chi attributes. That's the pelvic boost as a coordinated support gesture. I know what you're thinking now: *Aha! Busted! So the masters who show this are just bucking their hips. It's not a* dantian *thing after all!* That's a totally wrong conclusion. If you think like that, not only will you never master this stunt, but you'll also miss out on the profound attribute development the work can offer.

If you try to launch your object with a crude, forceful, and visually obvious hip-bucking, you may as well give up right now. Nothing's gonna happen. The object will remain sitting on your gut, or at most kind of slide down off it. There is zero chance you'll get the nice light popping launch into the air (like a fly ball) that way. Because hip-bucking is too muscle-bound and mechanical. This stunt requires some finesse and politesse and the pelvic engagement angle really hammers that home.

The pelvic boost is not a full beat behind the belly launch gesture. It lags, but by only a half beat. The relative timing of the two gestures isn't simultaneous, but neither is it full 1-2 timing. If G is the time of your belly launch gesture, then the pelvic boost is timed something like G + 0.03. Begin with the belly gesture and allow it to gently "pull" your pelvis very slightly upward. The hips are very softly and subtlety entrained during the launch. Bucking your hips will kill the whole thing. You must let the belly lead. The very slight, *almost invisible* pelvic motion cannot pre-empt but it cannot lag too much either. You begin with the belly and finish with the pelvis. It's almost, but not quite, one single gesture.

Getting the correct coordination of these two gestures (the main launch with belly and the gentle, slightly lagging pelvic boost) is the challenging part of this trick. And that's also where the learning potentially comes in. Maybe now you can see why my earlier discussion seemed confusing and contradictory.

On the one hand, if you take this as a muscular or purely physical performance, you won't be able to do it at all and you'll learn nothing from the attempt. Then it becomes nothing but a worthless distraction. On the other hand, maybe you can take my instructions seriously. Then you won't worry too much about showing anybody that you can do it.

You can treat it as a gentle, unhurried, mostly non-physical energy co-ordination challenge. In that case, you'll be able to achieve it with no problem, and, much more importantly, you'll get some serious insight into the nature of Tai Chi's *mind + body + energy* coordination.

Now, how do the actual hard waves play into all this? After all, the hard waves 'ride' on the breath, as previously discussed. Here's where the gut toss angle can expand the range of TAP training to bring it even closer to real Tai Chi. When you do the gut toss, all you need to focus on mentally are the gentle, relaxed, calm gestures – the belly toss and the entrained pelvic boost. If you stay calmly focused, the hard waves will coalesce naturally, on their own, to coordinate with the overt physical gestures.

When you're doing the gut toss, if you feel any kind of physical strain, pain, tightness or fatigue in your abdomen, stop immediately. That means you're doing it wrong. You're using physical effort. At the mo-ment of launch, your toss object should feel totally weightless. The launch itself should feel fun, breezy, easy. That's a technical guideline. If it feels any different, you're putting too much effort into it. This work is exactly like push hands in that you need to refrain from physical effort.

And that's the beauty of this gut toss thing. *It's conceptually equivalent to push hands.* Authentic Tai Chi push hands, just like the gut toss, uses no mechanical strength, only a 4-ounce *physical gesture* (e.g. a push) to focus and guide your *energy.* The gut toss works on exactly the same principle. Also, in push hands you don't need to mentally track the full ARC cultivation pathway. You just sense your partner's tension, touch lightly, begin the physical gesture with a calm mind, and the result takes care of itself. *This gut toss thing is the same.* That's the true training value of the gut toss. You don't need to explicitly concentrate, or even feel, the hard wave *per se* when doing the gut toss. If you stay relaxed and calm, the energy will focus itself and accomplish the task. Exactly as with the push hands gestures. The more basic TAP work you've done, the more internal energy you'll have feeding naturally into the toss.

The principles of *breath independence* and *minimal physical force* are the basis of success with this otherwise useless stunt. And those are exactly what you need for real push hands. This stunt can be either a worthless distraction or a deep teacher. It's either laughably shallow or infinitely profound. Your call which it's going to be for you.

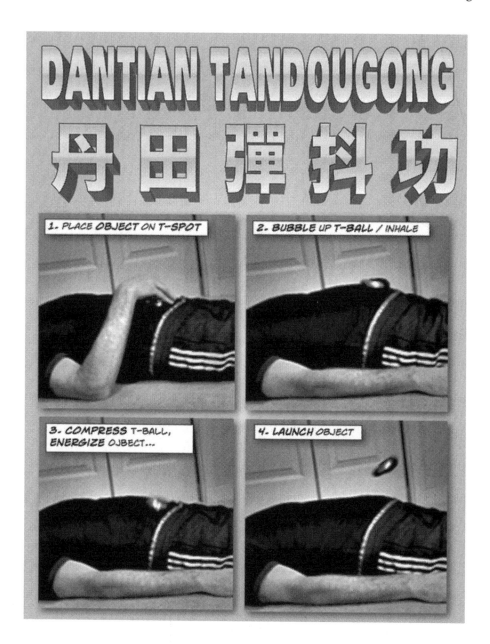

The Point of the TAP

When all's said and done, the purpose of the TAP is not to accomplish anything lying down, nor to toss rocks or locks. Eventually everything comes back to regular Tai Chi. Stand up and do your form. When you're in solo training mode, not demonstrating for YouTube or grandstanding for anybody, you know that the waist slightly leads in all Tai Chi movement. It's very subtle, one of the few concessions to physicality in Tai Chi. But you can use that for internal experience.

When doing your form, as you begin the waist turn that powers your transition to the next pose, try to trigger and really feel the hard wave pulsing through your torso. This isn't quite the same as the perpendicular version of the hard wave that you've worked with in the TAP. But you'll notice it far more quickly and strongly if you are doing the TAP regularly. The hard wave of the TAP is confined to the T-Ball. By contrast, when you do the form, you'll feel that same hard wave completely infusing, almost encasing, your entire torso as you turn the waist. This is called Old Ox Energy (老牛勁). It's truly amazing. When you can work consciously with this effect, it will totally transform your Tai Chi sessions.

As you continue working the TAP every day, you'll eventually realize that your body is something like 1,000% more charged with the tangible internal power than it was in your pre-TAP days. Suddenly one day during practice you'll realize that you really can feel the 'live' internal power bursting in your *tanden*. You'll be amazed from the moment you tangibly sense that. Then you'll tackle the daily TAP work with renewed enthusiasm. You'll never look back, and never give it up.

Chapter 3

SEALING THE ARC

The kernel of this section is the Hand Infusion Protocol (HIP). But before I get to your hands, I've got to back up for a deeper energy architecture overview. All my books are about the same thing: the *macrocosmic* energy process and pathway that you'll experience in three segments:

- **Accumulate** (in the *tanden*)
- **Rebound** (from the feet)
- **Catch** (with the hands)

That list comprises the invariant underlying energetic process of internal martial arts. It was fully vetted by the ancient masters, and is attested to in the Tai Chi and other classic writings. That's what all my work is built around. Talk about repetition! But there are many ways to skin the cat of ARC. All these different internal martial art 'styles' are just a preference of some historical master or teacher for *variant ways of moving the physical body*. In every case the mental and energetic process is wrapped tight around that same ARC core, 100% of the time.

The previous chapter went into great detail on the Accumulation phase of *tanden* development. Maybe you haven't yet felt very much directly from that work yet. I assure you that if you do the TAP regularly, every day, over just a few weeks, your internal power will be massively augmented. It will go far beyond what it would be without the TAP regimen. And you *will* feel that – maybe not today, maybe not tomorrow, but soon, and for the rest of your life.

The TAP is done lying on the floor, with the energy wave axis perpendicular to the physical platform (*tanden*). Now we're going to stand up again like proper martial artists. We'll experience the *tanden* energy vertically, raising and lowering it throughout the upright body. Just as the force and heat generated in the carburetor get extended through the drive train and converted to other kinds of energy, we'll now use the *tanden* to ignite other kinds of full-body energy experience.

From ancient times something like the ARC has been known as the royal road for energy work. Even though Indian yoga and meditation systems are best known for emphasis on the *microcosmic* orbit (torso and head circulation) there are many hints in the yoga classic writings that the energy surges up from the feet:

> *The goddess, having reached the abode of Shiva, the place beyond the Supreme Lord, satiated by the pleasure of enjoying that place and filled with supreme bliss, sprinkling the body of the yogi from the soles of his feet to his head with the dewy, unctuous, cool nectar. This is the secret yoga taught by me, O you who are honored by the master yogis.*
>
> - Khecarividya

Notice the directionality of that – '*from* the soles of his feet *to* his head'. That's the Rebound, which this chapter covers in operational detail. Another sutra cites the same direction of flow:

Focus on fire rising through your form
Upward from your feet
Until the body burns to ashes
But you remain.
    - Bhairava

What about 'points' (穴位) and 'meridians' (經絡)? In my past work, I've called out some especially useful points and channels. The most useful points for beginners are these four:

Dantian – lower belly
Lingtai – upper center of back between shoulder blades
Niwan – center of head
Daling – inner wrist

The *lingtai* is a special place of both amplification and also differentiation. At the *lingtai* point, the mass of energy surging up from the lower body in effect 'splits'. The more substantive (feeling) *yang* component wraps around the sides of the back and shoulders, seeking frontwardness. It also drills straight forward, through the chest to the solar plexus area. Meanwhile, the lighter (feeling) *yin* component of the power continues its surge up from the *lingtai* relay center. It ascends along the remainder of the spine, including the back of the neck, to and through the head. The *lingtai* energy point is also found in classical yoga teachings when they describe the kundalini power rising through the chakras (energy points).

    ... in the triple staff in the middle of the back, extending up to the
    juncture of the head and neck.
      - Kaulajnananirnaya

In other books, I've poured a lot of ink on the Rebound part of the ARC. I've provided dozens of drills and variations that engage your feet, legs and hips to activate your energetic *foundation*, the energy surging up from the soles of your feet. I've also pointed out the extreme emphasis on lower body (non-physical) *aiki* power taught by Japanese hyper-master Yukiyoshi Sagawa and how that precisely aligns to the classic Tai Chi teaching: *'power rises from your feet'*. That's covered in my book *The Aiki Singularity*. I can't rehash all the foundational Rebound stuff to the same level of detail in this book.

In this chapter, I'll cover the energy rising above the waist. I'll show how to activate the entire lower body foundational energy (which includes the slam-down from your activated *tanden*, the rebound off the soles of your feet, and the up-swelling that re-fills your lower belly *from below*. To get the most from this chapter, you may want to work with the foundation drills and Rebound energy as described in the other books. With that background, you're primed to instantly feel and appreciate this 'single mouse-click' activation of the lower body's energy, *as a one unit*. But first let's cover the power surging above the waist.

The Head

In an old film from Professor Zheng Manqing's New York school, he talks about the power's trajectory up your neck, straight through your brain, and then its frontward spread across and down your forehead and face. This too is part of the ARC.

The idea of internal power bursting up through the spine to the head is nothing novel. Since Vedic times, sages have taught and written about the *kundalini* power rising up the spinal channels. This Tai Chi version is a function of that same energy. I often get the question *'what is the difference or the relation, if any, between the Indian idea of kundalini vs. the Chinese internal energy concepts?'*

Short answer: *it's the same thing.* There's really only one spirit power. But it manifests in many forms for many purposes. It's like water which takes on infinite forms and flows. You can analogize it to a sailboat vs. a windmill. Viewed from one angle, they are the same thing: catching wind in canvas to perform work. Conceptually however they are distinct and have almost nothing in common. One is an static food processing device, while the other is a means of transportation and shipping.

The energy is the same, but your result will be shaped by the method, the expectations and the goal you apply. If you're into static meditation for long periods of deep introspection that takes you far from this world, you can mobilize the power as *kundalini*. That's your ticket to ride on a wild LSD type of mental trip. If on the other hand, you emphasize mobilization of the energy throughout your body as a tightly integrated permeation, with a properly 'martial' awareness and engagement with the physical plane, the energy will manifest more along the lines pioneered by the great Tai Chi masters. This martial arts mode is more properly compared to the mellow yet absolute bliss of heroin.

The sage seeks a sharp peak of enlightenment. The internal martial artist (well, this one at least) seeks a mellow summertime hammock of pure pleasure, without any sacrifice of sensual immersion or protective alertness in the world. But whichever road you choose, be advised that this power is a real thing. It is not just a word, or a bland cover term for some common psychological state that arrogant Western psychologists assume they have nailed. Nor is it a dry abstract philosophical thing. Whether you choose to explore it or not, it's as real as the center of the earth or the Mariana Trench or any remote but real location where people don't normally tread.

The Professor straightforwardly described the conceptually simple but practically difficult process whereby the rising energy blazes a path through your head.

Figure 3.1: Professor Zheng described the rise and descent of the internal power to his students.

What he's showing and telling there is the reality of the process as I've laid it out in my books. I noted in *Juice* that there's generally an over-emphasis on the crown chakra (百會 *baihui*). The crown chakra is lit up by the passage of the energy through the head. But every other head point lights up too. That's what has caused the confusion, along with the fact that people like a point that's easily identified with a clear physical correlate.

However, the whole crown chakra (百會) thing is actually a byproduct and sideshow to the main event, which is the pass-through from back of the head, straight into and beyond the *niwan* point (center of brain). This is the process the Professor is calling 'difficult' in that film. But it's not super hard, like winning a Nobel Prize or doing yoga's *kapotasana* pose. You just plug away with the right mental focus (gentle but persistent). As they say in Ashtanga yoga *"practice and all is coming"*. That works for Tai Chi too.

Here is how hyper-master Sun Lutang (1860-1933) described this above-the-waist ascension process in his Xingyiquan writings:

陽氣升於腦即丹書穿夾脊透三關而生於泥丸之謂也。

The yang energy rising to the brain is described in the classic dan-tian *training texts as passing up the spine, penetrating the three gates and manifesting at the* niwan *point.*

I've already explained that the head portion is really the *yin* branch but otherwise that's a good summary of the effect. In another writing Sun clarifies that the head is basically the lighter energy offshoot, as I've previously pointed out:

頭為稍節在外為頭在內為泥丸是也。

The head is the minor branch, with the skull as its outer energetic circumference, and the niwan *point as its inner centroid.*

Remember this is something you really feel, not another religious or philosophical thing. It's amazing and absolutely blissful, but you never lose touch with external reality. Once you feel the active suffusion of the *niwan* point, you're poised for the really fun part. From the *niwan*, the power flares outward as it projects forward onto your forehead, from behind, like a backlit movie screen. This is shown by another illustration that appeared in an earlier book. I need to retread it here because we're going operationally deeper now, and this is the launch pad.

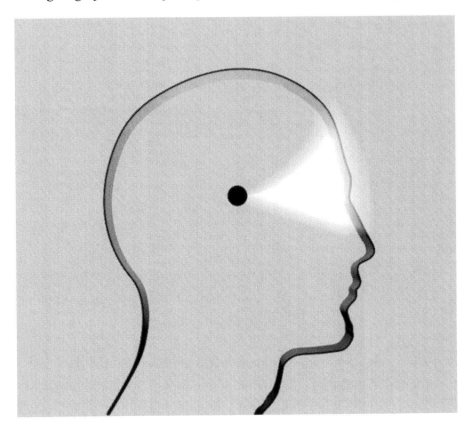

Figure 3.2: The power pours forward through the brain into your forehead from the *niwan* center point.

It may seem like I'm going in circles here, but bear with me. Everything comes together in one simple Tai Chi practice below. You already know it, but I'm going to take you to its next level by an easy road. The key with this head thing is that you need to sense the flare-out *tangibly* and *directly*. No abstraction allowed. No philosophical mazes or terminological dodges. It's like a powerful stream of warm water spouting up like a fountain from your neck, streaming through your brain, and then flooding out into your forehead like a big river entering a delta that drains to the ocean.

By now you should have the basic idea of the foundation (from previous work), the back split, and the head flow-through. The key is to whip these segments into a unified, simplified, optimal non-sedentary practice method – the Hand Infusion Protocol (HIP). Let's talk about an ideal body configuration for that.

When first beginning Tai Chi training, my teacher learned the form up to the Raise Hands pose very quickly, but then spent the next year doing basically nothing but that. His teacher didn't give him any more. I believe my teacher's astonishing internal mastery derived mainly from that 'static' interval, when he had almost nothing else to work on.

Figure 3.3: Raise Hands (提手) is an ideal Zheng Style Tai Chi pose for cranking the Hand Infusion Protocol.

The Hand Infusion Protocol (HIP)

I'm not a big fan of hyper-structuralism or over-focus on mechanics and physiology for internal training. That's never the main point. However, in the beginning you do need set the train car on the rails, after which you don't have to fuss too much about it. For any Zheng Style Tai Chi pose, my teacher emphasizes the following structural points:

- Relax
- Body upright (don't lean back, forward or sideways)
- All weight entirely on rear leg (front leg barely touches floor)
- Waist facing frontwards (not canted sideways)
- Wrists flat and straight, fingers gently and softly extended

For Raise Hands, you must keep 100% of your body weight on the rear supporting leg. Your rear palm faces your forward inner elbow. The front foot contacts the floor on the heel only. Keep a bit of comfortable space between your upper arms and your torso. As you stand, 'test' the front leg by raising it slightly off the floor from time to time to verify that your body and balance do not suffer any deformation at all.

If you can do everything above, all at once, you're good to go. After that, the only remaining structural thing is to sit low, bend the knee more, and create a nice acute angle at the inguinal crease (胯 kua) of the supporting leg. After my teacher corrected the five principles listed above, his main work on us consisted of exhorting us to sit lower and sharpen that inguinal angle ('bend the hip joint!').

But the above are only the grossest mechanics. We now need to work our way toward the internal space. The first thing to consider is the state of your gut. Remember what we talked about in the TAP chapter –

your belly is like a bag of water, not a block of ice. That's not super difficult when you're lying down comfortably for the TAP (though at first you'll be surprised how much unconscious tension remains in your abdomen even under ideal circumstances). Now in this more physically challenging Raise Hands pose, it seems harder for most people to keep the abdomen gently relaxed and feeling expansive. But it has to be done.

But what about the rest of the TAP? Should you be consciously working the whole BUBBLE thing while doing Tai Chi standing, or the form? The answer is no. Remember that the TAP and the BUBBLE are worked from *shavasana* (lying down). It's a powerful 'offline' training protocol. But Tai Chi is derived from a martial art. Apart from a few shared basics, such as the relaxed 'bag of water' abdomen, there is no *overt* overlap between the TAP and upright Tai Chi practice. Therefore you don't need to get into the full BUBBLE and TAP stuff when doing Tai Chi. Work on the other stuff coming up in the next section.

But what about *breathing* in Tai Chi stances and form? Even if we don't perform the full BUBBLE and TAP protocols while standing, is there nothing more to be said about breathing in Tai Chi? People love breathing because it seems like an easy mechanical bridge to spiritual energy. As part of the TAP, you've already worked with your breath and become more gently and unobtrusively conscious of it. Beyond that however, and particularly when doing Tai Chi stance work, it's best to breathe mildly, gently and naturally. Forget about breath for the most part. Once you're familiar with the HIP practice you'll naturally need to spend less and less time and effort on controlling your breath and adjusting your posture in the physical realm. It will become more of a pure energy practice. Drink down the following teaching from the yoga classic writings, as it applies equally to Tai Chi's internal energy work:

> *Don't die struggling to fit yourself to the pandits' knowledge. Understand that the supreme level is different, and reach it. Posture and*

*breath cause trouble. Minding these, day and night, you will die still
in the beginning stage of yoga.*
   - Gorakh, Sabdis 31

There is however one powerful add-on. It's more of a mental training
technique than a breath method per se, but I'll mention it now. As you
stand in any ZMQ pose, but particularly the Raise Hands we're focusing
on, you can use a mental image of your abdomen to accelerate the energetic concentration. Remember that mind generates and controls the
internal energy.

The 'bag of water' image is great for basic relaxation. Once you are somewhat relaxed in this area, you can add bit of (purely mental) structure
to your *tanden* work in this stance. That is what I call 'scaling'. That
is, scales as in lizard plating. Lizards and reptiles have a highly mobile
plating on their outer surfaces, including belly. For an image of breathing that concentrates the power (without the full TAP and BUBBLE stuff
which are only appropriate for seated or supine work) then imagine that
the surface of your belly is *plated* with these smoothly movable scales.

If your belly was plated like this lizard's body, you could feel the plating opening and closing slightly through each breath cycle. So when
standing, you can occasionally call that image to mind, as you continue
to breathe naturally, gently and calmly. Don't force your breath in any
way. Just become more aware of it. This lizard plating imagery will help
with that.

The 3 HIP Power Zones

The Hand Infusion Protocol requires you to pay some active attention to
two power zones, and if you can do that, you'll activate the final zone,
the hands, automatically for free.

Figure 3.4: If your belly was plated with these kinds of scales, you'd feel their movement against each other with every breath action.

The first thing you need to do is subsume and ignite the lower body power. It surges up from your feet, filling your legs and then completely permeating your lower torso, including hips, groin, lower abdomen and sacrum / tailbone area. Being able to perceive, control, and intensify this flow results from working seriously with the foundation and leg material in my other books. But if you're not familiar with those, that's no barrier, because the Raise Hands stance, all by itself, works powerfully to develop and deliver the lower body integration.

I'll assume that, in this Raise Hands stance, you can trigger and tangibly experience the Rebound effect of energy streaming up from your feet and filling your lower torso. The next thing you need to do is press the sacral button. Of course there isn't really a button there. The sacrum is just the bone at the lower back side of your hips, the area between and just above your sit bones. Pretend there's a low wall or object just behind that place, and (mentally) very gently press your sacrum backwards to barely touch it. There might be a slight physical accompaniment to this back-pressing ideation, but it's mostly mental.

This is where some of the mechanical principles that my teacher has stressed work powerfully to amplify the internal harvest of the work. It's common in Raise Hands, and its twin sister pose on the other leg, the same shape with a different name (手揮琵琶 Strum the Lute), to cant the waist somewhat sideways, It's a kind of blading the body. But that's not optimal for the internal effect we're now seeking. Don't do that. In the illustration, you will observe that Master Yang Chengfu's waist is bladed or canted. That's fine – at his supreme level he could do as he liked. But for us, it's best to orient the waist directly forward, as shown on the right side of the graphic.

Figure 3.5: The three power zones of the Hand Infusion Protocol.

You should establish a feeling that your sacrum is barely touching something back there, but not physically pressing it or leaning on it. As soon as you 'set' the sacral touch, the energy of your integrated foundation (feet, legs, lower torso) will blast up the spine. At the *lingtai* point it will branch, as previously described. The *lingtai* point is a broadcast or relay station.

The light *yin* form of the power will continue straight up through the back part of your neck and then curve through your brain, centered on, but not limited to, the *niwan* point. The *niwan* point is also a broadcast or relay point of amplification, much like the *lingtai*. So the energy will seem to fan out as it fills your forehead – from behind. It's a very interesting feeling. From there, just as the Professor teaches in the film snip, the energy descends easily through your face, neck and the front of your chest. It branches in the front on its way down, just as it did in the back on its way up, to fill your arms. The *yin* and *yang* components are now reunified as a torrent filling your arms. It feels absolutely fantastic.

As you stand, you can further amplify the flow by holding your head as though you are feeling a soft Nerf ball between your jaw and collar area. This optimal angle of head positioning is not something you need an aged lama in a Tibetan snow cave to reveal. That would be typical teacher fussiness but not necessary here. In fact it's counterproductive to have a teacher messing with your angles because you may never learn to create the right internal settings for yourself. So just gently experiment with this feeling of gently trapping a soft Nerf ball with slight pressure in front of your throat. As the energy pours down from the forehead, over your face and down the front of your neck, it will seem to 'inflate' the ball further.

You should experiment by very gently and slightly adjusting the position of your head and jaw, while paying strict attention to the *hand flow* that results. Is the flow choked or amped by any given small adjustment? It's like a throttle which you learn to control. More precise calibration leads to greater power amplitude. Become results based, not blindly following a teacher's aesthetic preference or a style's blind dictates. Feel it on your own so you can feed it on your own.

From the throat pour-down, the power continues to your solar plexus where it re-combines with the *yang* branch mentioned earlier and the unified power streams into your arms and hands like nobody's business.

The final power zone (hands) now comes into play automatically. If you have the right posture and the right gentle focus on the previous two power processes (sacral touch and forehead stream), the hands will fill automatically. This is only a description of what you'll experience, not something you need to actively 'do'. You just need to set it up right and then 'allow' it.

The power is attracted to the last of our 'relay stations' – the inner wrist *daling* points. Those are shown as white power centers in the graphic. These will collect the rushing power stream and amplify it as it sends the energy in to your hands. At first you'll probably feel only the throbbing and filling of the *daling* points themselves. Next, you'll become aware that the fleshy padded parts of your lower palms, immediately adjacent to the wrist seem to fill and suffuse with something. This sense of suffusion will get increasingly powerful in those areas, and will keep creeping forward through your hands.

The power is always attracted first to the beefier, more padded areas of your hands. Thus the famous *laogong* point in the center of the palm, which is the instinctive favorite of most dedicated but inexperienced Tai Chi and Qi Gong people, is actually the last part to fill with the real unified power. You can get great sensations there without experiencing the full HIP as I'm describing it. But there's a lot more that can be done. The final stage of the HIP is the energetic engorgement of each finger.

This HIP Tai Chi hand suffusion has nothing to do with the commonplace 'feel the static' exercise taught in every weekend 'Intro to Chi Gong' class on the planet. In that teaser drill, you are taught to hold your palms facing one another about six inches apart. You'll feel some tingling and light pressure, as though you're holding something soft and warm between your hands. This easy and fun effect is entirely on the *outside* of your hands. It is external qi (外氣) and can be felt by anybody in less than 5 minutes of work. The HIP is a far deeper operation. It's tightly integrated with your full body energy system (ARC) and takes a little longer to develop, because the internal power suffuses centrally from within your forearms, wrists, and hands.

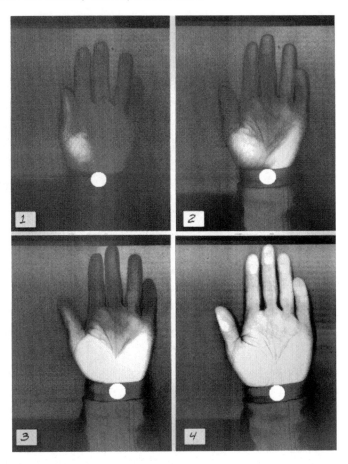

Figure 3.6: The stages of automatic HIP infusion of energy to the hands: from the *daling* circular point, spreading outward into the fleshier parts of the palm and fingers. Panel 4 represents the fully 'painted' hand.

Those who've worked with my Xingyi materials will note that the pattern of suffusion in Tai Chi appears different. From Xingyiquan's specific training shape for the hands and its energetic protocols, you'll feel a strong stream along the outer edge of the ulna bone in your forearms, outer edge of your hand, and your little finger in the outward direction. Then there's a crossover along the back of your hands, then a powerful return stream from your thumb along the inner edge of your forearms.

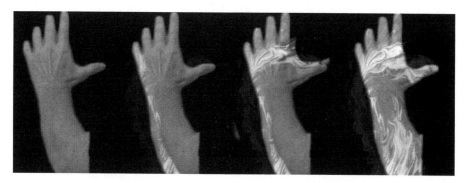

Figure 3.7: (left to right) Xingyi hand infusion: extends along outer/lower edge of forearm; crosses through back of hand; infuses thumb; finally returns along inner/upper edge.

In Tai Chi, the energy spreads forward and outward from the central relay area (*daling* points). In Xingyi, you'll generate a shape like an isosceles triangle with the point near your elbow and the base across the back of your hand.

This is not a contradiction. They are both training modes, helping you experience and learn patterns of precise calibration. Consider again sailboats and windmills. The basic energy is identical in both cases. But the workflow differs hugely, depending on the desired goals and outcomes. The key thing is to get full control, on mental command, of at least one of these training flows and states. From there, when you're really convinced of the reality of this stuff, you'll want to play with different protocols. Just as once you've got basic control of balance and movement on a skateboard, you want to experiment with many variant tricks. The more different patterns of energy you can call up, control and calibrate at will, the deeper and more powerful your permanent energy charge will become.

Sealing the ARC

Sealing the ARC is where you establish a kind of shortcut for the power. Instead of concentrating on the full flow, you work it down your front for the most direct possible linkage. The protocol begins as before:

1. Sacral Touch
2. Forehead Pass-Thru
3. Hand Infusion (passive)

You stand for two or three minutes on each side, feeling the effect. The operation is like a dead man's switch, in that the stream of power will keep running through you as long as you gently maintain consciousness of the sacral touch.

Figure 3.8: Sacral touch

But if you're really feeling it, you can take it another step forward and apply another turn of the screw. To do that, make sure you understand the basic HIP already described. Not only must you understand it, but check that you're actually feeling the stuff streaming into the meaty parts of your hands when you stand. If you are actually feeling that, every time you stand, you're ready to seal the ARC.

For sealing the ARC you can re-deploy all the HIP infrastructure you've already worked up. That includes the Raise Hands stance as the best place to begin. Set yourself up as the HIP specifies: sacral touch, forehead flashout, and hand infusion.

But we now add Sealing the ARC. It's mostly mental. All the previous ARC work, including the HIP, energetically connects your *tanden* to your hands – but indirectly, taking the long way round. That's essential in the beginning. You must experience and clarify the full ARC as a prerequisite. When I say 'directly' connect *tanden* (the start of the ARC) to hands (the ARC terminal), you should understand that they're always connected indirectly anyway, via the full ARC. That doesn't change even with this sealing protocol. In fact it only intensifies further. What changes is your depth of understanding and speed of engagement. But it isn't possible to do this Sealing without having gone through the full ARC channel and also the full HIP training already given.

First, review the discussion of the T-Spot in the first section of this book. We're going to need that, so hopefully you've developed some working experience with the energy and sensation of concentrating on your T-Spot. Then, you need to have some feel for the inner wrist points (*daling*) also covered earlier. Finally, we *connect* those things, while standing as in the HIP. The bridge between the two is your mind, using an image of long (cooking) chopsticks.

You will stand in Raise Hands, exactly as for the HIP, as before. Feel the flow-through from your feet, the forehead flash-out and the hand infusion. Now, use your mind. You already know the exact location and

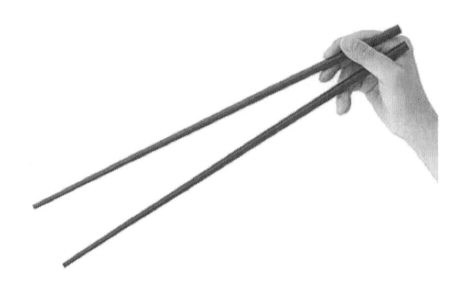

Figure 3.9: Use the mental image of long chopsticks.

feeling of the T-Spot. Imagine a pair of long chopsticks. Each stick has one end pressed gently against your *daling* point (one per wrist) and the other end pressed into your T-Spot, exactly the abdomen point used in the long pole drill for T-Spot ignition. Feel that the ends of the chopsticks are almost breaking the surface of your skin and digging into your tissue – but that this is done gently. That's another contradiction with immense training value.

Stand and feel the two chopsticks lodged onto the T-Spot, and gently maintain them in position. This is awkward to do with *real* chopsticks, due to differing distances in the hand positions. But it's also unnecessary. Now you'll understand the value in the earlier work using an actual pole against the T-Spot. Having had that experience, it will be fairly easy for you to mentally recreate the sensation. That re-creation of the energetic triggering will drive imagination toward reality.

Figure 3.10: Sealing the ARC: the (mental) chopsticks gently press from your inner wrist on each side directly into the T-Spot.

After doing this Sealing work on both sides for a few minutes, stand upright, feet shoulder-width, weight 50-50 shared equally on both legs. This is the Preparation Posture of Tai Chi. You'll be amazed at the gigantic power surge that results from this simple Sealing work.

I understand that you really want something much more exotic than *this*. It looks so *plain*! You've *seen* that pose already! But isn't that reaction interesting? We want something more difficult, sexier, saucier, and spicier. Something more complicated, with lots of internal *structure* and a dozen preliminary steps of *process* and *procedure*. It's odd because most people will never actually engage in long-term practice of any complicated regimen. Most people will just scan the diagrams and nod approvingly, even as they toss such a book aside. Yet anything that looks *too simple* is scorned without even a trial run, even though it's way more effective and powerful than most exotic methods.

Persistence with the TAP, the HIP, and the Sealing will have a cumulative effect, day by day making the energy more alive, more available to your mind, and vastly more resonant in your body. Perhaps some day you'll reach the incredibly refined level of my Tai Chi teacher, who is able to concentrate the energy so powerfully through his hands that he can make the center of his palms puff up like a popcorn pan – truly an amazing feat to see.

Figure 3.11: Tai Chi masters can hugely and visibly expand their center palms, like a popcorn pan top exposed to heat.

Even if you don't reach that level of visually dynamic display, you can learn to 'paint' your hands internally with the energy, and experience that effect to your own satisfaction. Painting or coating the hands is the full manifestation of the HIP. You'll actually feel that your entire hand surface is coated with a thick layer of fingerpaint, and that, when in motion, you are smearing it all over any surface or partner. It's a really fun phenomenon.

Related to this is *rippling* your hands. This will not normally develop into a visible/visual effect. However you will be able to feel inside that the entire 'fingerpaint' surface of your hands (everything from the *daling* point, across the palm, into the inner surfaces of fingers, knuckles and finger pads) is vibrating and *rippling* with the internal energy. It's basically a flattened out and broadened version of the hard wave periodic vibrations that I've described with the elbow/wrist drill. But now it manifests across the surface of your hands. You can learn to ripple your hands, from the inside.

Reaching this point, you can now *return* to your classical forms with serious insight. *This* stage is precisely what these forms were created to exploit and experiment with. Many people blindly practice classical forms as fitness routines, dance spectacles, or museum displays of archaic 'combat' techniques. In my view, none of those things matter much. But the classical forms offer a truly peerless internal energy experience when understood as such.

For example, the Chen Style Old Frame 1st Routine is not for internal energy beginners. It's far too athletically distracting. A beginner is not supported in learning relaxation by this level of physical demand. In fact, such a form works to unintentionally *undermine* a beginner's relaxation and energy sensing. The same can be said of practically all classical internal training sets, at least what's available to most of us in the modern age.

Figure 3.12: Double Jump Kick (踢二起) of Chen Old Frame 1st Routine (老架一路). This kind of thing distracts beginners from the quiet relaxation essential for sensing the real internal power.

However, by using the methods I've outlined in this book, you'll get to the point of personal insight and tangible experience with the internal energy. It's a real thing, distinct from all other work on your body, mind and soul. When you've begun to engage with it, if you then return to some of these classical training systems, you'll be amazed at the hidden genius they embody.

For example, when you perform your Chen Style Old Frame 1st Routine, you'll be bowled over by the energy experience. It gives you the chance to extend, rotate, concentrate, fold, spindle and blast your internal flow like nobody's business. A form like that is a priceless practice tool.

If an elaborate and highly nuanced from like the Old Frame 1st Routine is too much overhead for you in any dimension (performance time, performance space, learning it, remembering it, athleticism, etc.) there are plenty of simpler options available as you work to bolt this basically non-physical energy onto your physical body dynamics.

One of the best is classical Yi Quan (意拳 - mainland China, not the USA Bay Area version). Even just a single Yiquan pose will be very revealing and fascinating to practice, once you've gotten some tangible mileage from the HIP work. That pose is called "Descending Dragon' (降龍樁). In addition to Yiquan, this is commonly found under different names and minor variations in a dozen styles of Chinese martial arts. While some masters work this one at a very low height, with their butt practically scraping the floor, you can get the full energetic benefit of it from the mild or mid-level version as shown.

Figure 3.13: Yiquan's Descending Dragon for 'painting' the surface of your hands with energy.

If we were doing actual Yiquan with this, I'd now have to cover a whole slew of complex visualizations and imaginary pulleys, gears, springs, levers, walls of diamond and other interesting exotica. But for a maximal energy hit, you can work much more simply with plain mind, extension, relaxation, and grounding.

Relax your abdomen - remember the *bag of water* thing. Press strongly into the ground with the lead leg and foot, while – seemingly paradoxically - completely relaxing into the long body extension. Look toward your rear heel. Notice that this pose highlights, emphasizes and privileges the *daling* (inner wrist) points with a kind of extrusion. It's the best configuration known to me for explicitly engaging the *daling* points while gently encouraging you to sense the full body infusion (abdomen twist and spinal extension).

The tricky thing is to work the four elements of MERG (Mind, Extension, Relaxation, Grounding) without going hog wild, as we humans tend to do. For example, with 'Extension' - sometimes people work crazy hard on systems that involve hard torqueing of ligaments and tendons (sometimes called 'wringing the towel'), which they believe can be done without tension. But every attempt at that kind of forceful twisty/stretching stuff, fashionably cast as working the tendons and fascia, always ends as just plain old muscle tension. And tension nullifies you at the starting line.

Most importantly, as you do Descending Dragon pose, put your mind into the 'fingerpaint' surface of your hands. You'll feel they are painted or coated with energy. Do each side for a minute or two, then stand quietly upright and relaxed, feeling the hum and throb of the power throughout your body. The Descending Dragon pose has a rare value. If you do the mild version as pictured, you can bake in all four key ingredients (MERG), while also explicitly triggering the *daling* points – thus leading to the painted hands effect. This pose allows you to trigger all that without crossing the line into counter-productive forceful hyper-twists and useless towel-wringing.

Towel-wringing sounds great on paper but in practice 99% of the time it devolves into plain old muscular force. It's far better to relax and sense your way into the energy rather than trying to force your way in using fancy words like *fascia* as lipstick on the tension pig. If you really love twisting and wringing yourself so much, why not play with the big dogs - try your hand at the Ashtanga 2nd Series pose *pasashana* (noose pose). That'll seriously wring out your towel.

Once you are internally activated, whether you play with Yiquan or Chen Style Tai Chi or even the Praying Mantis form charted in the first chapter of this book – all of them will be totally transformed by your explicit control and amplification of the real internal power.

Now, in case you still aren't weirded out enough, here's something else. As a teen, I got intensely energy-centric classical Xingyiquan training. After my teacher directly showed me as much as he could, he wrote out a cardboard-bound reference book ('The Manual') of Xingyiquan internal principles and practices, from basic to super advanced. I've talked about that before. But there's a lot in there that has taken me years to experience for myself, without even thinking about trying to teach it. Doesn't help that it's all couched in old-school literary Chinese. I'm proficient in that, but it doesn't make these extremely abstruse topics any more tractable.

Anyway, one of the phenomena that my teacher wrote about in the advanced section of that manual is what he called 'Eye Wheeling' (眼輪 *yanlun*). It's only recently in the past few years that I finally grokked, via direct experience, what that was all about.

Physically it's simple. Stand normally upright, feet shoulder-width, body relaxed, arms naturally by your sides. Now, gently rotate your eyeballs as through tracking the second hand on a clock right in front of your face. Clockwise or counter-clockwise doesn't matter (later, when you've actually felt the effect you can experiment with specific parameters like that).

Now hang on! I know you're thinking this is another goofy thing like those Internet 'throw away your glasses' scams. But it has nothing to do with that.

The human body is basically encased in a kind of energy shell, roughly ellipsoid in shape. With this exercise, we are going to work with and experience that directly. As you gently revolve your eyes, if you have enough full-body charge and if you are sensitive enough, you will feel the energy shell, as a perfect circle, revolving around both the *edges* of your body and partially *within* your body. It's such an amazing thing, as though you are encased in a Ferris wheel, yet your physical body is stationary. Only the energy shell moves, but it grinds really powerfully, in direct correspondence to your eye movements, as though tethered to them.

99% of readers might not yet have enough full-body charge, and aren't relaxed enough to feel this. So you'll be there rolling your eyes, feeling like an idiot and you won't experience anything. Sorry. I don't know what to do about that, but I can relate, since for decades that was me. I began to think that this section in the training manual was some kind of abstract Taoist thing which (unlike all the rest of my teacher's stuff!) wasn't meant to be felt literally, directly, and viscerally. Well, I was wrong. Bang, one day I was able to feel it and it really blew me away.

You may wonder whether it has any training value. I could respond: *No, but as things with no training value go, it's one of the best* (thanks Woody Allen!). But that would be wrong, because if you can acquire this level of charge, sensitivity and control, and if you actually practice this (gently and briefly, don't go hog wild with it), over time it has the power to massively amp your energy and control.

I told you this would be weird, didn't I? Maybe just remember this section but put it aside for a few years while you work the other energetic foundation stuff. There are various protocols in Chinese classical *neidan* meditation that involve eye concentration and movement in various complex linkage patterns. But I haven't seen anybody describe this extremely simple, direct yet powerful level of tangible eye linkage via such a straightforward mechanism. It may be out there somewhere though – I have seen and read a lot but not yet *everything*.

While I'm on the subject of The Manual (Xingyiquan training secrets), I want to mention another of its weird but very important teachings. That is the training idea my teacher called 'Sleeving your Legs' (袖化腿). I think a better name would be to invert it, as 'Legging your Arms' - but whatever.

I'm sure any reader of this book has worked kicks on pads and mitts. If you've done much pad work with a good Muay Thai player you have more than just an armchair idea of the vast power difference in legs vs. arms. The legs are easily more than double in power. Of course, that's ordinary physical power, generated through plain old athletic muscle – not the subject of this book. But we all have a good intuitive feel for this power differential (just by living years in a human body). It's very intuitive and that universal intuition can be exploited in an incredibly useful internal power amplification drill.

Even though I use the world drill, it's an essentially mental operation. You do need some kind of performance framework to run it but the actual work of it is mental. It's extremely powerful once you get the hang of it, but that may take a long time. Though I was introduced to this almost 45 years ago, it's only in the past few years that I've begun to seriously perceive its effects and have come to hugely value it.

As you do some stance, any stance actually, or any movement later on, you project your leg power directly into your arms. I mean, you literally imagine that your legs *are* your arms. Somehow just imagining that your arms are sleeved into your pant legs, or vice versa, that your legs are inserted into your coat sleeves, is enough to supercharge your entire arms with internal flow, from shoulders to fingers. It's not so easy but extremely and tangibly powerful when mastered.

This is described in The Manual in terms of Xingyiquan stances and movements. But because those are an entirely separate training topic, I'll suggest something better for most readers. I have found that the absolute best and simplest *pose* to work the Sleeving effect is the Zheng Style Tai Chi pose called Left Wardoff (and you can do the same on the mirrored Right side also, of course). For some reason, this pose both engages the legs in just the right way, and also positions the arms optimally to improve the odds that you'll be able to work this for real.

Figure 3.14: Zheng Style Tai Chi's Left Wardoff is an ideal pose for training 'Sleeving Your Legs'. Note that the arm curvature angles somewhat reflect the leg shapes.

But the sleeving work can (and should) be done in motion also. For motion, you could use any familiar form or drill you may know, such as those previously mentioned. Personally, I've found through extensive experimentation that even though I was introduced to this in a Xingyiquan context, the best way to get an initial feel for the dynamic version of it is through the classical Chen Tai Chi silk reeling drills. These are commonly taught in other styles too. I included the version of Silk Reeling that I learned on one of my commercial film tutorials. But to avoid getting screeched at for cross-marketing or up-selling or SEO-shilling or whatever, I'll merely suggest that you search online for the terms 'Chen style silk reeling'. Something decent will pop up, and you can follow along with that.

My job here is not to teach you those commonplace mechanics, but to emphasize this subtle but incredibly interesting mental protocol. It's simple in a way, and subtle at first, but revolutionary once felt. The simplest way to put it is that you mentally imagine or feel, as you stand or move, that your legs 'are' your arms. That somehow your legs' power is perceptible and usable *directly inside your arms*. Even imagining this as a *physical* thing (the leg/arm muscle power differential discussed above) triggers this *internal* power effect. As you move, feel your legs then transfer that feel to your arms. Or just mentally reattach your legs themselves to your shoulders. Bang! Instant super upgrade of internal power – even though it's essentially working with a physical symbol (legs).

This Leg Sleeving work is what finally got me to an operational understanding, or at least a training comprehension, of what Yukiyoshi Sagawa meant with his unrelenting emphasis on leg and lower body power – *yet not as muscular units or mechanical levers.* This Sleeving concept is one of the most effective pry bars into the lower body non-physical power sourcing effect that I called the *Aiki Singularity* in another book. Other such pry bars will work better for beginners who are just learning to relax. But once you've begun to sense your charge, the Sleeving work is one of the most effective things you can practice to engage it further.

Chapter 4

PUSH

不可勝在己 可勝在敵
Your defense lies in your own hands,
But the enemy defeats himself.
　　　- Sunzi

Before we get into the more technical push drill stuff, let's look deeper at the Tai Chi training significance of the leading quote above. Everybody throws around stuff like that - *the enemy defeats himself*. It's generally interpreted as a moral or even spiritual thing. Morihei Ueshiba, the founder of Aikido, famously stated:

When an enemy tries to fight with me, he has to break the harmony of the universe. Hence at the moment he has the mind to fight, he is already defeated.

That's beautiful. And it covers the same basic territory as the Sunzi quotation above. But I led off with Sunzi's quote from 'The Art of War' because, although we don't know whether Sunzi did Tai Chi, we do know that he wasn't all that spiritual. He comes across as a practical man, and I'm using his quote to make a practical point.

Without getting moralistic and spiritual, it's a simple *technical* truth about Tai Chi that the opponent *must* defeat himself. Otherwise it isn't Tai Chi. It may be something great, but it's something else. That's because Tai Chi does not use physical force in its signature 'push' (按) technique, nor in any other. So what moves an opponent, when s/he is pushed by a real Tai Chi master? The master's push gesture turns the ignition key. But that gesture is *not* the physical force that moves the opponent.

The push gesture is merely a trigger that detonates the opponent's own internal tension. Underline that sentence! For some reason people have trouble understanding or even remembering it. Yes, *qi* or *jing* are real energies – but they do not function as direct mechanical levers. What would that be – *telekinesis*? That's crazy talk – too woo for school.

Dig if you will the picture: the master uses his internal energy only to trigger (detonate) the partner's tension. The resulting explosive release of pent-up, unconscious tension causes the opponent to move himself, whether by a little or a lot, depending on how much tension the master chose to set off with the trigger. The situation is similar to atomic bomb operations. A thin neutron-source initiator rips through a fissile mass, setting off an explosive chain reaction. The beryllium initiator on its own is not capable of destroying a city. It's only the trigger.

This's why real push hands looks so fake, making it hard to demonstrate for an audience. Of course, external grappling skill can be entertainingly exhibited in a Tai Chi configuration. But the real use of internal always looks fake. If it doesn't look fake it isn't the real thing.

Because the opponent is moving himself! Which sounds identical to the condition of um... actual fakery. Fakery would be when the opponent purposely and deliberately moves himself, throwing himself around to make the teacher look good. There's plenty of that nonsense in all internal arts. The problem is that even a real internal master is triggering that same thing – the partner's own inherent physical force, by the tension detonation mentioned above. In the eyes of the casual observer, that appears identical to the fakery case. But it's not. Because the *real* response is not under the opponent's voluntary control. The tension is detonated at a time and place and manner of the master's own choosing, not the partner's. This is the crucial difference between real and fake push hands outcomes, though they look about the same.

Anyway, take this principle of *triggering* or *detonation* to heart, or you'll end up missing the entire point of push hands and Tai Chi. Be energy centric at all times. The take-home is that, quite apart from all the spiritual mumbo jumbo, the 'enemy' quite literally overthrows himself. It won't always work with everybody you face, but over time the more solo energy training you do, the more naturally and powerfully you'll find yourself applying this type of effect.

Now let's get technical. Here's another highly illuminative quote from our Master Sun ('Art of War'):

> 凡先處戰地而待敵者佚，後處戰地而趨戰者勞。
>
> *Whoever is first in the field and awaits the coming of the enemy will be fresh for the fight; whoever is second in the field and has to hasten to battle will arrive exhausted.*
>
> - Sunzi *Bingfa*

That nicely hits the concept of this next drill. To such an extent that I could call this the "Art of War" drill. I could also name it "Go-No-Sen" (後の先), from the classic samurai sword teaching of '*starting after the enemy but arriving before him*'. This idea is even more explicit in another observation from *The Art of War* : 後人發先人至, '*though starting later, arrive first.*' We love these training slogans but rarely do you find an explicit, safe, yet non-choreographed training protocol that brings it all to life.

My Tai Chi teacher has been renowned as a top master of push hands and related skills. He always particularly emphasized this section's drill for timing and sensitivity, as an expression of the essence of interactive Tai Chi. We could call it by any name, but I feel the Japanese phrase above is short, pithy and accurate so I'll refer to it as the Go-No-Sen (GNS) drill. In fact, it has something of the look-and-feel of the first micro-second of a sumo match – but with the aim of slipping or neutralizing your partner's push, not opposing it with strength.

A and B face each other in mirror opposite front-weighted Tai Chi 70-30 basic stance. One partner is limited to offense, the other to defense. It's a very limited type of offense, just one straight push at a time. There is no follow-up, no combinations, no wrestling. Mike Tyson once said: *"One, two, three punches; I'm throwing punches in bunches. He goes down, he's out. I'm victorious."* That is perfect boxing advice - always follow up to the end. But here, we're deliberately limiting the action so we can concentrate on a subtle Tai Chi attribute.

Let's call A the pusher and B the defender. They begin from stillness, in the setup mode. There are two variations of setup. The Basic mode involves both partners full engaging both arms. They can touch each other's upper torso, chest, shoulders, upper arms forearms and/or hands freely. There is no physical position for initial arm placement that offers any advantage. If there were positional advantage it wouldn't be an internal energy practice.

In Advanced mode, the pusher does the same preparatory positioning as in the Basic mode. The defender however begins with arms hanging straight down. Of course, the arms can be raised and engaged as needed (or not) to deflect the incoming push. But Advanced mode requires greater sensitivity and (soft) reaction speed. The end result in both modes is the same from the defender's point of view: the incoming push should be neutralized without foot movement.

A takes a turn by gently extending a single push. This is not an attempt to smash B onto the wall. It's only to get B to move his or her foot. Foot movement is a sign of tension in the body that could only be relieved by taking a step (or being knocked over). That's sufficient to work on the core attribute. No need to turn it into a bar fight.

Figure 4.1: Sample ways to setup: 1. Basic mode (A or B can touch anywhere on partner's upper body and/or arms); 2. Advanced mode (defender's hands unengaged)

A gets one push, and then – regardless of outcome – he retracts and resets. B only defends and – regardless of outcome - does not counterpush. When the turn is over the players reset for another try. Usually A makes three attempts (as pusher) and B attempts to neutralize each of those (as defender), with a reset after each attempt regardless of the result.

Perhaps you can see the genius of this down-scaled push-hands drill. It preserves just the one iota of "objective reality", in that it is *non-com-*

pliant. It's not one of the patterned, choreographed dance routines emphasized in some Tai Chi classes. The pusher makes every sincere and legal (e.g. no stepping in for mechanical leverage) effort to move the defender. The defender will make every sincere and legal effort to neutralize the push while avoiding foot movement. If the defender is relaxed enough, or if the pusher uses too much force, the push will fail as the neutralization succeeds. Otherwise, the defender will have to move at least one foot to keep balance.

Since each engagement is limited to only the one action and single reaction, it's understood from the beginning that this can't lead to a brawl or other overly intense commitment to outcome. Regardless of the result on any given turn, the players calmly reset and go again. To keep it interesting, after three attempted pushes by A, the roles are reversed for the next three turns, and so on.

From the pusher's point of view, the goal is to minimize use of physical force while still getting the result. If A uses even 1 ounce more force than necessary, assuming B is sufficiently relaxed, then B will never be moved. Push with no more force than you'd use if standing on ice. If you were standing on ice, how much force, strength and pressure would you apply to your partner? Anything over 4 ounces of power is going to send you sliding backwards. Try feeling that you're standing on ice, so you can't use more than 4 ounces of pressure (or less). Alternatively, you can imagine how you'd push if standing on only one leg.

Tai Chi master Yang Banhou (1837–1890) wrote as follows:

合則放發云不必凌霄箭涵養有多少一氣哈而遠

When I connect to the opponent, I move him away, but I don't try to launch him into the sky like an arrow. With a slight puff of my intrinsic energy he'll move far enough.

That is a perfect expression of my teacher's emphasis on "*just move his foot*". Or I could say, just cause him to move his own foot. Work gently with precisely calibrated space and time. You should aim for limited effects rather than grandstand plays. Working in this way, you'll learn a lot more a lot faster.

The lowest level of engagement is a physical **push** (用力). The next level is a **probe**, that uses a bit of force, like a bat emitting sonic energy. The response you get to your probe corresponds to listening energy (聽勁). The highest form of engagement is merely to **place** your hands in contact with the partner – with no force at all. Your hands are silent. His tension seeks out your hands. It comes to you. This corresponds to understanding energy (董勁).

Figure 4.2: Don't *push* at all. Just *touch* with energy. Don't try to blast him, just make him lose balance and move his feet.

On each reset, it's important to avoid any pre-emption. Defender B cannot respond, or attempt a neutralization, until A's push has begun. Even if B's response seems lightning fast to an onlooker, it must begin at least 0.000001 seconds after A's initiation. There's a definite feeling to this on both sides, so after some practice both will understand when this condition is being met, no matter how tightly the time is shaved. That is the meaning of 後發先至 – *starting later but arriving earlier*. It's truly an ingenious, educational and fun way to develop your sensitivity. This practice leads directly to the highest Tai Chi sensing abilities: *tingjing* (聽勁) 'listening energy', and *dongjing* (董勁) 'understanding energy'. Most students have heard of those attributes but have little specific idea of how they can be trained.

The pusher's offensive repertoire, the range of physical gestures, is seriously curtailed. A is limited pretty much to a straight push, applied to B's arms, torso, or upper hips. After all, if you as the pusher are using light internal energy as you should be, why would you need fancy or tricky techniques to simply get him to move himself?

Figure 4.3: Pusher must apply a single gentle, straight line, simple push with one or both hands. No tricks, no twists, no techniques, no combination. Pusher does not try to hurl defender to the wall, but only tries to get him to move one or both feet.

Figure 4.4: Neutralization by defender. No special technique, just minimal redirection or jamming with a turn to either defender's open side, or closed side, or redirect upwards. The same defenses apply whether the setup was Basic or Advanced mode.

The defender (B) has more flexibility in his or her neutralizing response. B must try to 'defend' himself' by removing, jamming or redirecting the push, not just passively root or hope for the best. The defender should actively attempt to defuse the incoming push, but always in accordance with the fixed restrictions of the drill. Over time, defensive neutralization will happen naturally in accordance with the incoming push. It may be rooting, or redirecting with some kind of turning or yielding gesture, or it may be a kind of nearly invisible 'jamming', with hardly any apparent physical gesture at all. The specific shape of the defense hardly matters, because it appears organically.

The important thing is that over time defender B becomes sensitive enough and calm enough to wait without responding until pusher A's gesture has begun to 'cross the starting line' – even if only by a nanosecond. B must learn to feel the very instant when A has irreversibly committed – no matter how softly A's push is initiated. B must then neutralize as soon as possible after A's gesture begins. Eventually B will feel the initiation in A's mind before anything happens at all. Reaching that stage, defender B still must not physically pre-empt, but B's neutralization is guaranteed to succeed, even though it begins after A's push. A was defeated before beginning, by emitting some kind of tension signal – as long as B is 'listening' carefully enough to catch it.

Figure 4.5: The defender (left) tries to under-hook the pushing arms of pusher (right). Under-hooking the pusher's arms, as an attempt by the defender to get below the push, only works against a forceful physical push. This common tactic will not work against the true internal.

My partner for this photo sequence (260 lbs vs my 140 lbs) stated the following, unsolicited (there were witnesses): *"It feels like I'm beaten from the get-go."* I quote this not to blow my own horn but to remind you – that is *precisely* the point of this work. That is the very definition of Go-No-Sen. It's not pre-emption, it's *'late start early arrival'*.

This need not be the only kind of push hands training a student engages in. Everybody should freely indulge in the normal rough and tumble 'pushes in bunches' (free-style pushing) whenever they want. But this is deep foundational work that will greatly enhance your sensitivity.

I'll conclude with more about *structure*. Everybody loves that word for emphasizing physical mechanics and components, maybe because it has such a nice engineering feel to it. I frequently hear through the grapevine that Tai Chi cognoscenti diss my push videos, saying things like: "Yeah, maybe Scott moves them, but look at that lousy/crummy/non-existent/etc. *structure* on him!" I always laugh out loud when those kinds of comments get back to me. Because they are making my own exact point for me. If my structure is that bad, then obviously structure isn't the key element in push hands. The power must be coming from ... *elsewhere.*

The elsewhere effect is triggered by the light energy that transfers on contact between your hand and your partner's body. This is the *yin* energy of light touch, which I've called *yinjection* in other books. There's no special secret to understanding that. This simple Go-No-Sen drill gives you all you need in a training framework. Just remember that it is neither your physical force, nor even your internal force working like a tractor beam, that moves your partner. *He moves himself* at all times with his own unconsciously tense reactions. Your only job is to get out of your own way, let the *yinjective* energy do its thing to trigger him.

If at any point in this drill, whether you are pusher or defender, you find yourself getting sweaty or a little short of breath, stop and rest. Not because there's any danger, nor am I worried about you over-exerting yourself. If you're in the boxing gym you should be sweating buckets and your corner guys should be pouring water into and over you. But this is Tai Chi. If you get red in the face, or you sweat, or pant, I know with 100% certainty that you're using physical strength.

In that case, even if you're "winning" the drill (as pusher or defender) it's totally meaningless. You're just using some unholy combination of strength, size, mass, technique and/or tricks. This drill, above all others, has been crafted to eliminate most of those irrelevant factors. But no drill is perfect. It's still possible to beat the system by use of strength, size, and technique, especially with a lesser-skilled partner. But don't do that. Why cheat yourself? Fortunately we have the signs of physical exertion as the simple diagnostic that will warn you, just as effectively as if my teacher himself were standing right there supervising. Touch lightly and trust the process.

I mentioned in the TAP chapter that the gut-toss (of an object off your T-Spot) is conceptually identical to push hands, and that the gut toss can even be a kind of solo practice mode for push hands. How does that work, given that in push hands, your partner moves himself with his own un-consciously tense reaction to your light *yinjection* energy? After all, the rock or lock that you throw in the gut toss, as an inanimate object, has no reaction or sensitivity at all. It seems like a contradiction, but you'll understand it through practice. The gut toss and push hands both train the fundamental attribute of applying a light, almost non-physical ges-ture to achieve an outsize external result (the object toss or the uproot of a partner). This requires learning a certain kind of mental control that both practices can offer. The technical details of the two practices differ slightly however.

The uproot of a live partner applies the *yin* energy of *yinjection* which triggers his own power to work outside of his control. The rock or lock toss is a momentary concentration of the hard *yang* wave. That's the lower *yang* power, which with its vibration can have minor but visible material effects. It is *not* telekinesis or any goofy woo like that, because it absolutely requires the coordinated 4 oz. physical force of the nearly empty gesture. I call that *yangjection* - *yinjection*'s grubby little brother.

This shouldn't surprise you. In earlier videos I have shown how the hard wave vibrations can affect your body physically, and how those vibrations can be felt by another person. The hard wave, as the bridge between physical and purely energetic realms, does have material effects. The gut toss stunt is applying that power momentarily to move a non-sentient object, which cannot be done at all with the pure *yin* power. The pure *yin* power does not work against '*men of iron, stone or wood*' (as Yang Luchan nicely phrased it). The *yang* energy of the hard wave isn't really combatively useful. But it can contribute to throwing an object, if initiated with the right kind of physical gesture. The hard waves suffuse your abdomen with a concentrated charge that helps to power the physical effect. Even through the implementation of the gut toss is coordinated through a slightly different format of internal energy than push hands, both practices can develop the same fundamental attribute of 'applied relaxation'. Eyes on the prize!

Chapter 5

THE LIMIT

世人不知內勁為何物。皆於一身有形有象處猜量。或以為
心中努力。或以為腹內運氣。如此等類。不可枚舉。皆是
拋磚弄瓦。以假混真。

*Ordinary people have no idea about the internal power. They assume
it's merely the body's shape or physical structure, or that it might be
purely mental concentration, or abdominal breath mechanics. They
go on guessing randomly about it, but all that is totally false, like
handing out a brick when a ceramic tile was requested.*

What else can I say? I've covered more than enough to get you going.
I've done my best to explain the foundational internal attributes
of Tai Chi, and to target them with drills, and to expedite their development with context and insight. Go have fun with it. A street dealer
doesn't lecture you on the molecular psychopharmacology of the substance. He hands you a sample: "Hey man try it." Don't get distracted
in the beginning by style wars, historical contention, theatrics, athletics
or even combatives. Take it slow and trust the process. The slower the
journey the more the traveler sees.

THE END

Made in the USA
Lexington, KY
17 February 2018